The Tattered Tapestry

The Tattered Tapestry

A Family's Search for Peace with
Bipolar Disorder

Tom Smith

with Kevin and Karla Smith

iUniverse Star
New York Lincoln Shanghai

The Tattered Tapestry
A Family's Search for Peace with Bipolar Disorder

Copyright © 2005, 2007 by Tom Smith

iUniverse Star
an iUniverse, Inc. imprint

iUniverse books may be ordered through booksellers or by contacting:

iUniverse
2021 Pine Lake Road, Suite 100
Lincoln, NE 68512
www.iuniverse.com
1-800-Authors (1-800-288-4677)

Because of the dynamic nature of the Internet, any Web addresses or links contained in this book may have changed since publication and may no longer be valid.

ISBN: 978-1-58348-385-5 (pbk)
ISBN: 978-0-595-89411-6 (ebk)

Printed in the United States of America

We dedicate this book to Karla. We only wish it were fiction.

Kevin and Karla at Paradise Point, July 2002

Contents

Acknowledgments

More people than I know, and certainly more people than I can remember, contributed to this book. This story is a part of the personal history of the Smith family, and we are the products of thousands of relationships, some of whom we can name and many who are uncounted but influential, unidentified but significant, unnamed but a part of the fabric of who we are as individuals and as a family. We are grateful to all of you.

Within this general but genuine acknowledgment, Kevin, Fran, and I want to publicly identify some of you who helped shape this book. Many of your names appear in the text because you lived this story with us as it unfolded and before we knew we had to record it. Thank you for your presence then; we know that these relationships continue to enrich us.

More specifically we want to thank Tom Hart and Kathy Fischer, both published authors, for reading an early draft of the manuscript and encouraging us to proceed. Fr. Charles Rubey is the courageous and compassionate founder of LOSS (Loving Outreach to Survivors of Suicide), which published excerpts of this text in *Obelisk*, the insightful newsletter of this grief-reducing ministry. We are grateful to him for his personal empathy and for telling part of our story. Fr. Bill Hitpas demonstrated his compassion during these events and remains an exemplary pastor today. He also read an early version of this material and offered some perceptive comments.

Sharon Smith and Pat Petkowski read the text and urged us to seek publication. Thank you. Before we submitted the text to the publisher we formed an editorial review committee comprised of Janie

Bloomer, Margie Jones, and Emily Sherbert. This competent trio, each with her own set of skills, critiqued and improved the logic, text, format, and grammar of the story. We truly appreciate your commitment and contribution to the final product. Robert Grimm, my nephew, and his wife, Karen, designed and created the original book cover. We are sincerely grateful for your time, talent, and dedication to this project.

Fran chose not to write for this book, but she breathed and grieved every word of the text as she offered suggestions and support for its publication. The three of us want to publicly express our appreciation to and for each other as we publish *The Tattered Tapestry* and direct the Karla Smith Foundation. Our experience, personalities, and skills differ but we unite in our never-ending love of Karla, and our hope for a balanced life for all people who love a mentally ill person or who lost a loved one to suicide. That is our vision and *The Tattered Tapestry* is ultimately about sharing that vision.

Finally, we are grateful to Karla, who graced our family for twenty-six years.

Kevin, Karla, Fran, and Tom enjoying a family cruise in July
2002

1

Paradise Point, 2001

In 2003 I took my third trip to Paradise Point in three years. My wife, Fran, and our friend Margie joined me in climbing the steep, wooden steps to the sky-tram. It's a cable-driven, glass-enclosed compartment similar to a ski lift, and it takes seven minutes to reach the top of Flag Hill. Memories of my two previous rides surfaced quietly while we chatted about the scenery, the heat, and the uniqueness of the ride itself. When we reached the top and stepped out of the tram onto the platform, I stopped and stared. There was the same gorgeous Flame tree, still lush with scarlet blooms, that our son, Kevin, had captured so well with his digital camera the year before. During our first two visits, we had been inspired and elated by this vista. This time, however, we looked on all this beauty in silence and tears.

Paradise Point nestles comfortably near the peak of Flag Hill, seven hundred feet above sea level, with a commanding view of the city of Charlotte Amalie and the harbor for St. Thomas, U.S. Virgin Islands. Our massive cruise ship, the *Adventure of the Seas*, looked sleek and delicate from this height, and the view of the city, the small islands in and around the harbor, and the gently rolling Caribbean were captivating. The scene was postcard perfect.

I was captivated by Paradise Point two years earlier in the summer of 2001, when Fran and I took our first Caribbean cruise. St. Thomas was near the end of our itinerary, when we were tired and wanted to spend some time in a peaceful and inexpensive place with some local

1

color. After shopping in Havensight Mall at the foot of Flag Hill, we thought that a quiet ride to the top of the hill would be just about right. For me, that short journey delivered more than I had expected. Fran liked Paradise Point too, but she didn't feel the appeal of the place as profoundly as I did.

Some people are attuned to the ambience of places. They sense the vibes, intuit the spirits, and reverberate with the tones of locales. They claim that certain cities possess somber and threatening auras and that other cities exude warmth, creativity, welcome, and serenity. They are sensitive people, aware of their surroundings and willing to absorb the emanations of a place. Generally, I am not one of those people.

Why Paradise Point captured me is still a mystery. When people ask me about it, I mention the view, the veranda, the margaritas, the setting. No one questions me further; people simply accept that it is a special place for me. But it bothers me that I can't pin down the attraction more completely. I only know that this place has somehow entered my soul.

Other people have similar experiences of intense rapport. For me, Paradise Point prompted that experience, but any other place, or an event, or a relationship, or a moment of personal enlightenment, or a spiritual awakening might do the same for others. Ultimately, I believe all these experiences are spiritual because they touch us so deeply. For me, God breathes a spirit into Paradise Point, and I caught a wisp of that spirit.

I was ripe for Paradise Point. The cruise itself, the stops at previous ports, and the rapidly building euphoria of the previous five days had all set me up for something special. Most of all, Paradise Point symbolizes peace for me. It's more than quiet contemplation at the feet of an accommodating creation. It's peace with a promise that all things will come together, that both the world at large and my personal life have meaning and are interconnected. It's a vow that the stress of work and the strain of misunderstandings, unfulfilled expectations, and periodic boredom will melt into an endless beach of soft sand, cooling breeze, and the comforting waves of welcoming waters.

It's not that I feel Paradise Point is an oasis within a generally arid and chaotic world and that spending a little time there is a refreshing break from reality. The peace of Paradise Point extends in all directions, moving outward through the mountains, forests, skies, and seas and transforming all things into beautiful acceptance and boundless creativity. It paints all people with their best smiles, in their most flattering poses, even as it highlights each person's uniqueness. Its active serenity invites people to accept their individual greatness as well as their destinies as parts of a community. Its peace simply reflects the heart of God.

I didn't experience this peace as unrealistic optimism. I know now and knew then that life mixes beauty with fear, virtue with vice, and joy with overwhelming sorrow. There are holidays and horrible days, soul mates and strangers. Paradise Point does not deny the underside of life. But it insists that good triumphs over evil, trust outlives suspicion, faith erases despair, and love does, in fact, conquer all. It gives me a glimpse of what could be, along with the assurance that what could be, will be.

I wanted to keep my sense of rapport private at first because it seemed too extreme to share, too personal to translate, too unique to describe. In time, however, I changed. I wanted to share it, but sparingly. I feared that giving it away too easily would diminish and demean what I had experienced and reduce it to a mere travelogue. I felt I needed to invite others to share a similar experience. Perhaps to verify my reaction, I wanted someone else to experience it somewhat as I had before I talked or wrote about it. Perhaps I needed to fill in some of the images. To expand the core. To discover the basis. To celebrate the vision. To share it with someone like Karla.

My hope is that everyone has his or her own Paradise Point, an experience that radiates the promise of peace and weaves together some of the many threads that make up our lives. Without a Paradise Point, life is more difficult than it needs to be.

2

The Cycle Begins

As a child, in high school, and during her first year and a half of college, Karla was energetic, smart (in some areas, actually brilliant), involved, beautiful, and open to multiple life options. Her specialties were English literature, speech, drama, dancing, philosophy, theology and, above all and including all, writing. Math interfered with her 4.0 GPA, but she generally got Bs in the subject, even though she didn't like it or see the point. Her life plans changed often. She intended to get a master's and PhD, probably in English Lit, or counseling, or fine arts, perhaps after some years in the Peace Corps and/or backpacking through most of the world. The future was open, and she was going to live life fully: intellectually stimulating, many close relationships, a library of classics, and lots of music with a message.

After a long college search that included multiple campus visits and an overriding desire to find the school that would "let Karla be Karla," she fell in love with the intimate surroundings and freedom of Incarnate Word College in San Antonio. The San Antonio River Walk was a favorite additional feature, and she did well academically.

But after one year, she wanted a change. Several factors led to this decision, most notably Incarnate Word's lack of an exchange program that would allow her to study in Europe. She had always been adventuresome, and her desire to study in Europe fit her personality perfectly. Another factor in her decision to leave San Antonio was the breakup of her three-year relationship with her boyfriend, Mark.

Mark had just graduated from college in Colorado and was planning to move to San Antonio, but they decided to end the relationship and he found a job in Colorado. She was brokenhearted.

While she was at Incarnate Word, she had an experience that we were never able to fully assess. In spring of 1995, she went to a party at a friend's apartment in San Antonio. Karla waited outside a closed bathroom door for several minutes. Finally, she knocked on the door and heard no answer. She opened the door, went in, and discovered the dead body of a classmate's sister. The young woman cut her wrists, fell, and hit her head on the bathtub. Karla had talked with her just thirty minutes before she found the body, which she immediately knew was lifeless. She locked the door and sat on the floor of the bathroom for a few minutes figuring out what she needed to do next. She left the bathroom, had someone guard the door, shut off the music, and told everyone but the girl's sister and a few close friends to leave. She then called the ambulance and told them what she discovered. The ambulance and police arrived quickly and determined it was a suicide, commending Karla for the way she handled this terrible crisis. She saw a school counselor and came home the following weekend in order to deal with the trauma. I had asked her a number of times over the next few years if that experience had any lasting impact on her, and she always said no. But I still have my doubts.

All of those factors, plus the limited English Lit courses at Incarnate Word, led to her transfer to Oklahoma State University (OSU) in the fall of 1995. The first semester went very well—she loved her classes, lived in Stout Hall (the dorm where many of the English Lit crowd lived), and became active in a variety of on-campus groups. She especially enjoyed Papyrus, the club that wrote and edited a poetry magazine, and Amnesty International, which gave her an outlet for her activist views on some world issues. She also reconnected with some of her friends from high school who also attended OSU and developed some new relationships as well. To me, it seemed like an appropriate and wonderful college extension of her high school years. She was maturing into adulthood at an acceptable pace, and her future, though unclear as to some specifics, seemed promising.

The First Signs

Early in the second semester, January 1996, there was a noticeable change in her. She gradually lost interest in the same classes that ordinarily stimulated her and in all her relationships. She became sullen and withdrawn. We noticed it in her regular phone calls, but she said she would snap out of it soon and get back to her usual active self. A few weeks later, she complained about an inability to complete a paper for one of her classes. The professor was Dr. David Patterson, a brilliant man, admired by many students including Karla, and a leader in the Stillwater Jewish community. The assignment was to write a paper on Martin Buber's book, *I and Thou*, a book that I value and I knew Karla would love. The insights, wisdom, and language of this classic treatment on relationships captivated her to such a degree that she couldn't put any of her reactions on paper. She couldn't just "do the assignment;" her reflections needed to match the power of the book itself. She was unable to produce that quality of work, so she was unable to write anything.

More than likely, a growing depression sabotaged her ability to cope with such a personally challenging task. Dr. Patterson tried to help her, but ultimately nothing and no one was able to bring her out of the sadness and despair. By the beginning of March she dropped a number of classes, was taking an "Incomplete" in a few others, and was unable to continue. She came home to Broken Arrow.

The next month was grueling. Her depression deepened, and periodically she would lash out at us for something or another, expressing anger followed by more withdrawal. We made arrangements for her to see a counselor and a psychiatrist.

While she battled her illness, we (Fran and I on a daily basis, her twin brother, Kevin, who kept in close touch from Saint Louis University where he was majoring in Business Management, and other family and friends who also worried about her) battled our reactions to her. We were puzzled, fearful, angry, hurt, wishing, worrying, irritable, condemning, hopeful, disappointed—emotions that came and went, often simultaneously, always present in some combination. We all dealt with it differently, sometimes well, sometimes poorly.

I did not know what to do, or even how to feel. My love for her explodes from the core of who I am. I loved before the birth of the twins, but those births forever altered not only how I love, but the very nature of my love. The "I" who loves is forever, unalterably, proudly, gratefully, and humbly a father, one who helps create life. Most fathers, I suspect, have similar feelings. The fact that many of us share these feelings does not change the intensity nor minimize the impact of fatherhood. The twins rearranged the molecules of my soul.

As Karla slid into her depression, I tried to comfort, encourage, and guide her. She was appreciative, but I was basically powerless. Feeling powerless was not a new sensation. As the twins grew through childhood, adolescence, and toward young adulthood, the tug between my control and their independence was evident, as it is in all families. They call it "letting go," a fair enough term, but I always wanted to know where the "going" was headed. Determining boundaries, limits, curfews, and behavior for teenagers is essentially slippery. It's never really determined, and it must change regularly as the kids get older. Mixed in with that process is an inevitable collision with powerlessness, an expectation that my words or actions would have a predicted effect which, in fact, doesn't happen.

But the powerlessness in the face of Karla's depression was devastating. She and I always enjoyed talking with each other. We had mutual interests: philosophy, theology, literature, writing, and, in her earlier years, speech, drama, music, and a love for words. Even when we had some conflicts, usually about curfews or money, we were connected. But when her bedroom became her world and her bedspread turned into the walls of her prison, she couldn't or wouldn't respond to me. I would go back downstairs, dejected, puzzled, and unable to fathom the sad-eyed silence that stared at my questions, my words of encouragement, and my "I love you's." It was not the stubborn, silent defiance that showed up occasionally when she was in high school. This was a blank nothingness, a serious commitment to not being there—or anywhere. I couldn't deal with it, especially when it went on for weeks. I got angry at her, at her illness, at myself. Fleeting but intense anger. Anger born in frustration and fueled by expectations. Where was "my favorite little girl friend"? Why can't we at least talk? Why isn't the medication working faster? How could this happen to her? What did I do wrong? What really brought this on? Should I have been stricter with her—or, conversely, more permissive? Were there early signs and, if so, did I miss them? Could I have done anything about it? Why can't my love for her ease her pain and control the illness? Where is this all heading? Are there better doctors, counselors, hospitals? What will insurance cover?

I couldn't answer any of these questions—or dozens more. Advice from doctors and counselors was helpful but not satisfying. Confusion and worry stalked me everywhere. And overriding every other emotion, infiltrating every feeling, invading my mind, and strangling my heart was this pervasive presence of helplessness. I was powerless. I couldn't do anything to help my beautiful, intelligent, charming, ambitious, delightful, loving daughter. Nothing I would do would stop the onslaught of the illness. Doctors and counselors always commented that our family's commitment to Karla and our willingness to support her was extremely important. Perhaps, but, in the final analysis, I remained powerless.

Fran had similar feelings, and together we tried to console and guide our daughter and support each other as we grappled with a world we never imagined and hoped would end.

Recovery and Relapse in Europe

Eventually, the combination of medication, counseling, and family support brought her back from the abyss. As the Oklahoma sun warmed the earth, Karla gradually escaped the coldness of her depression, and her natural warmth also emerged. She restated her desire to study in Europe and, after many consultations with her counselor and psychiatrist, we all agreed that a year studying at the University of Utrecht in the Netherlands could be good for her. She made arrangements with OSU and left in August. By then, she was recommitted to school, interested in living fully again, and confident that the next stage in her life would be exciting and valuable.

She arrived safely (she always was a fearless traveler), met some people who quickly became her friends (Judith in particular), and was enjoying the adjustment to the city and University of Utrecht.

But there was a complication. In October 1996, she was able to come home for a visit and while she was in Tulsa, she met Aaron (not his real name). Aaron intrigued her, with his intelligence, charm, commitment, life story, and the fact that he was a practicing Jew. Karla was very interested in Judaism at this time, and, typically, her interest was not just academic. She wanted to belong. She was attracted to Jewish teaching and history, and longed to know more about the Torah and the Holocaust. Aaron was a personal doorway into all of that. This devotion, coupled with his personal qualities, captured her heart uncritically.

She returned to Utrecht and shortly thereafter Aaron joined her. Supposedly, he was on his way to Israel to join a Kibbutz, or the Israeli army, but he never left the Netherlands. The relationship that started so quickly began to deteriorate, but Aaron remained in Utrecht. Karla became fearful of him, school, the city, and her friends. She relapsed into another depression with her dark thoughts and paralyzing fear tying her, once again, to her bed. She had access to medication but became erratic in taking it. We were getting bits and pieces of what was happening to her, but she was half a world away, and we didn't get many of the painful details until much later.

After a tumultuous year, Karla was unable to finish her course work and finally came home in the spring of 1997. She was breaking up with Aaron. A pattern was developing: her depressions and, later her mania, were always accompanied by an unhealthy relationship with a man. Whether the relationship came first and contributed to her illness or whether the illness led her into the destructive relationships, I will never know. But over the years, the nature of her relationships with men was a good indicator of her mental health. I wish I had discovered that pattern earlier.

Her time in Europe was both a relief and a concern for me. It was a relief because I didn't have to deal with her depression on a daily basis as I did during those long spring and summer months of 1996 when I was constantly on edge, not knowing what to expect, trying to monitor her depression, worrying about a relapse, unsure of her mood, unable to make plans but still hoping she was coming out of it. Often I wasn't aware of my own tension since it became a routine piece of everyday life. I was reluctant at first to support the study in Europe, but after she left I felt some relief. We heard from her regularly, and we were aware of some of the complications, particularly with Aaron, but it wasn't like being involved with her daily.

Later, after I learned some of the details of her life in Utrecht, I felt guilty. I had convinced myself that "things were basically okay and that her problems were minor" but, in fact, they were almost a repeat of her spring depression, with the added fear and complication of Aaron to make it even worse. Why couldn't my hope for her and in her override her depression? My sense of powerlessness returned. But she was now an adult and making her own decisions. Despite her illness, her life was her responsibility, a perspective she regularly pointed out to us.

"I Am No Longer a Poet"

The gradual darkness continued. By the middle of May 1997, Karla was still living at home, and she was desperate. Fran was principal of a Catholic elementary school just a mile from our home. Karla called both her and me at work to tell us good-bye. Fran, with her secretary, hurried home and found Karla in our bathtub, drowsy, but awake, from all the pills she took. A note on the bathroom mirror written with lipstick said: "I am no longer a poet. I have lost all my words." Fran was frightened, but quickly got her to the hospital where they pumped her stomach. I arrived a little later. It was her first suicide attempt, and it scared us all to the core of our being. From then on, the possibility of suicide haunted us, always lingering ominously in the shadows of our souls. Once she went "that far," it was permanently etched in our worried minds. That memory never goes away.

In the spring and early summer of 1997, she was hospitalized twice, tried a few jobs but couldn't hold them, and made some new friends—some of whom were not the best for her. The depression was never far away, even when she was in the hospital and "getting well." There were more doctors, counselors, and medications. I worked at American Airlines at the time, and my insurance covered much of her treatment until she was no longer a full-time student. Then the full expense of her illness hit us very hard. After much consultation with her counselors, other medical and financial professionals, we followed their advice and let the state assume primary financial responsibility for her. We remained closely aligned with all her treatments and counselors but avoided going into bankruptcy ourselves. I still wonder if we made the right decision.

In November, she moved to Madison, Wisconsin, for seven months in order to enroll in the University of Wisconsin, but she never established residency and, after a series of jobs, she came back home in May of 1998.

Energy to Burn

In the summer of 1998, Karla's mood changed dramatically. Her energy had returned. She worked out of a Temp agency, moved into a different apartment, and increased her social life. She met some kindred spirits (most notably, Lonnie) at a restaurant in Tulsa called Perry's. A small group of "truth-seekers" met there almost nightly to discuss their views on spirituality, politics, philosophy, and Eastern theology. Karla was an animated participant in these sessions. She was excited about many things, felt great, and even took a class at the Tulsa School of Metaphysics. She was always a writer and penned the following sonnet about the professor of her class:

"His eyes are bright. They lock into my own,
As if transmitting knowledge via thought.
I will not take his answers, though, on loan,
For they are his, and I could use them not.
He's full of explanations of the mind,
And so was picked to teach us how to pray;
But I might guess they didn't try to find
A soul whose humble grace would show the way.
With flourish he expounds on unity,
As if he thought that we were just like him.
One glance at his raised chin and lecture fee
Suggests, instead, he thinks us rather dim.
Beset with questions of the universe,
I find that asking experts must be worse."

Her energy and ideas were accelerating, and I began to suspect that she had no brakes on this runaway train. Most of her focus was on developing a free university she called Tapestry. The idea was that she would gather friends who had a skill or some special knowledge (ranging from judo to poetry, ceramics, calculus, and computer programming) and these friends would teach classes for free. She would then invite all of Tulsa to participate, with a special invitation to the homeless, the addicts, and the people on the fringe of society. Teachers and students would be united in a spiritual communion that would heal and elevate them all to another level of awareness, compassion, peace, and social action.

I remember meeting her at a Denny's restaurant one evening. She was recruiting me to be one of her teachers and this particular

Denny's had become her office. She had notebooks full of lists, diagrams, arrows pointing in all directions, and multiple bullet points all outlining Tapestry. She kept talking, explaining, describing, even telling me details about the building she would rent to house her free university. When I interrupted to ask a few practical questions like funding, commitment from other people and recruiting, she dismissed these issues with a flip of her long blond hair and a promise that Lonnie would handle those minor concerns. She even had plans to "take Tapestry on the road" with an itinerary that included Houston, Austin, Milwaukee, and anywhere else where she might know someone. I left her that night exhausted and very concerned.

Around that time she met another man—a computer whiz recovering from an unusual neck injury. He was breaking up with his wife who had left town with their two teenage children. According to Karla, he also accidentally witnessed a drug deal in a park and was on a hit list of a drug gang that she referred to as the South American Mafia. This whole story is still vague and confusing to me, but what is absolutely clear is that Karla believed it and was deathly afraid of this Mafia. As her thinking about Tapestry became more delusional, her paranoia regarding this Mafia became more acute.

On her 22nd birthday (August 7, 1998), she invited us and twelve of her friends to her favorite coffee shop, Gold Coast, and gave a birthday presentation about her life. She was certainly an accomplished public speaker (winning numerous prizes in both grade school and high school in speech and drama contests) but her content on this night was inappropriately revealing, and we were embarrassed by some of the things she shared about herself. Afterward we talked with some of her friends who also felt she went too far. Karla, on the other hand, felt great about it and was still promoting Tapestry.

By September, even she recognized that something was wrong. But she refused to enter a hospital voluntarily, and we could not admit her unless we could demonstrate that she was an immediate physical risk to herself or to others. Her delusions and paranoia were not enough to commit her. During a period when she was a little calmer, she agreed to visit her Uncle Tom and Aunt Kathy (Fran's brother and sister-in-law) in Seattle. Both of them are counselors and had demonstrated their love and concern for Karla many times. Karla also felt a special connection with them. She wouldn't fly because she was afraid the Mafia would trace her name in the airlines' computers. She decided that the bus would be a better way to travel.

We made all the arrangements and put her on a bus in Tulsa with confidence that everything was in place. But we didn't count on the extent of her paranoia. By the time she got to Tucumcari, New Mexico, she was convinced that the Mafia was on the bus. She got off, left all her clothes and money on the bus, and checked into a motel. The next morning I got a call from the Tucumcari police asking me if I would pay her $35 motel bill. From their description, she sounded very delusional, definitely paranoid, and totally unstable. I asked what would happen if I didn't pay the bill, and they said that she would probably be admitted to the state mental facility in Las Vegas, New Mexico. If I paid, she would be released immediately. Trying to keep her safe, I refused to pay.

What happened next is still not clear. Karla later claimed that she was isolated, tortured, and mentally, emotionally, spiritually (but not physically) raped while she was in jail in Tucumcari. We talked with the police regularly and, of course, there was no hint of any mistreatment. Two days later, a judge ruled that she should be admitted to the Las Vegas hospital in New Mexico.

While the circumstances of her admittance were not what I preferred, I was relieved that she was finally in a mental care facility. Her month stay there finally provided an answer to her dramatic up-and-down behavior of the past three years. Karla was officially diagnosed with bipolar disorder, the newer term for what was previously called manic depression. Since this term was a new word to our family's vocabulary, we researched the illness intensely. The more we read and studied, the more certain we were that it was a correct diagnosis. At least, we now finally knew the enemy.

Karla did not accept the diagnosis and certainly not the remedy. On her way home from the Las Vegas Mental Health hospital, she quit taking her lithium, a common and necessary medication for bipolar individuals. Within the week her mania reappeared and since she was home with us, we saw her erratic behavior up close. We called Parkside, a mental health facility in Tulsa, and they encouraged us to bring her in. We developed an elaborate ruse, including the help of Rosemary, a nurse friend of ours, and my history of lower back pain. Karla came along, believing I was going in for some back pain consultation. Meanwhile, she claimed she was getting personal messages from the radio, and her messages agreed that she should come with us. Once we got to the hospital, we were able to admit her, but it was not easy. She became angry and resisted, but it was clear that she needed to be there, and a shot of Haldol, a drug to control psychotic disorders, calmed her enough to process the admittance.

A few days later, another judge approved her admittance to another state mental hospital, this time in Venita, OK. At the court hearing, Karla politely informed the judge that Thanksgiving was coming soon and she would be eating turkey, dressing, cranberries, and pumpkin pie at the Smith home in Broken Arrow, OK. The judge smiled and promptly sent her to Venita. We (Fran, Kevin, and I) visited her in the hospital on Thanksgiving and we prayed a genuine prayer of gratitude that she was safe and making progress. Our Thanksgiving dinner that evening was a little less than festive, but we were hopeful.

Two weeks later she was released and moved home again. This time she stayed on the lithium, and the symptoms of the mania were thankfully gone. On the other hand, our bipolar research warned us about the coming depression cycle.

Kevin had graduated from Saint Louis University in May 1998 with a business management degree ... minor in communications. He took a good job with Andersen Consulting (now called Accenture), the world's largest business and management consulting company. He lived in St. Louis on the weekends, but worked on a year-long assignment in Houston during the week.

On January 2, 1999, I started a new position in the Pastoral Services department of the Catholic Diocese of Belleville, Illinois, my hometown. I had worked at American Airlines for over ten years, and I wanted to get back to church ministry where I had begun my career. Fran was still the principal of a Catholic elementary school in Broken Arrow and was committed to completing the school year in June, when she would join me in Belleville. Karla was adjusting to life outside of mental institutions at our Broken Arrow home.

A Return to Depression

In early January 1999, the depression returned. Life seemed to be going nowhere for her, and her bedroom became her private, cold cave again. The deepening darkness led to Karla's second suicide attempt. While she was alone at the house one afternoon, she went into the garage, started the engine on her car, opened the car windows, and expected to die slowly. Fortunately, as she sat alone in the garage, she changed her mind just in time to escape a lethal dose of carbon monoxide. Later that night, she told Fran about the attempt and, once again, Karla was back in the hospital in Tulsa with severe depression. This time she was released into a living center that monitored her daily activities but allowed some freedom. She did well enough in this environment and by the end of January, she was accepted into a program that monitored her moods and behavior but allowed even more freedom. She seemed a little better.

Research has shown that many depressed people are most dangerous to themselves when they are coming out of a deep depression. When they are in their worst depression, oftentimes they simply do not have the strength to commit suicide. When they get a little stronger, a little more stable, but retain the suicidal thinking, they are extremely vulnerable. Karla lived this statistic. On February 3, 1999, she was still depressed but appeared to others to be improving. Not so. This time the darkness led to her third suicide attempt, and her closest brush with death. While her roommate was away at class (the same class Karla would not get out of bed to attend) Karla took over hundred prescription pills. As her overdosed, unconscious body sprawled on the bathroom floor, her roommate miraculously returned to the apartment to retrieve a textbook she forgot. There she found Karla and made a frantic 911 call. Karla was rushed to the hospital, put in an emergency room for seven hours, and then into intensive care overnight. Doctors claimed she survived by the matter of one hour.

She was admitted into a psychiatric ward in Tulsa for the next three weeks. Fran saw her as often as they allowed. I drove in regularly in order to visit. By this time Karla had been in so many institutions that she was somewhat calloused to the routine, the group sessions, the staff, and the whole setting. But as she came to the end of her stay, she softened, accepted the value of inpatient care, and willingly transferred into another program that was partial hospitalization, a little more freedom but with twenty-four-hour supervision. After a month she moved again—this time to a halfway house where they required each tenant to get a job or attend some program away from the house. They found a combination of meds that seemed to work for her, and she took them faithfully. Her life was gradually coming together and the healthy Karla began to blossom again. She started back to school, beginning with summer sessions just to see if she could handle it. She did beautifully, and in September she studied in Poland and continued to improve. As the months went on, it became clear that she was back on track.

During those first six months of 1999, I was severely conflicted. My new position in the Belleville diocese was going well, and I truly enjoyed getting back to church ministry. But I also felt like I abandoned my suffering daughter and my wife who was on-site to support her. The timing for my move could not have been worse. I called both of them often and visited regularly, but emotionally I was torn apart. I wanted to be there, to see Karla immediately after her suicide attempts, to encourage her as she entered and then progressed through the various programs and housing arrangements she was in. Part of it was the brute need to protect my only daughter, to assure her that she was okay and would be even better, to support her and Fran as they struggled through the bare, raw reality that our daughter attempted suicide three times. Even though my feelings of helplessness undermined my desire to help and protect her, even though my mind told me that I probably could not do anything about her suicide attempts and her hospitalizations, even though I knew my love would not make much practical difference in her recovery, I still wanted to be there. Just to be there. To see her up close and to talk to her face to face. The four hundred miles between us punished me with stubborn, unrelenting distance and a daily, sometimes hourly, reminder that I deserted my daughter in her time of greatest need.

On the other side of my psyche, I felt invigorated by my new position. The people I worked with and for were committed, friendly, effective, and fun. We shared a common vision of what we wanted to accomplish. It rapidly became the best work situation I ever experienced.

I was also in my hometown after twenty-six years of being "away." Kevin lived in St. Louis, just a half-hour drive from our home, past the Gateway Arch and Busch Stadium in St. Louis. My sisters, in-laws, aunts and uncles, numerous cousins and relatives of varying degrees and varieties of relatedness all lived within an hour's drive. And my mother was in a nursing home in Mascoutah, just fifteen minutes away. Seeing her regularly during her twilight years was a reward I will always treasure. After all those years in Iowa and Oklahoma, it was also a delight to meet grade school classmates, high school friends, and people I lived with, studied with and became a young adult with. Someone said you can never come back home. They were wrong.

Fran joined me in June 1999 and accepted a principal's position at Queen of Peace Catholic elementary school. We bought a home and started our new life together in Belleville. My guilt for being away from Karla during her crisis subsided because Fran and I were together again and because it seemed Karla was getting better. The home we bought has a finished, walk-out basement that we furnished and which could easily become a semi-separate apartment in case Karla would eventually live with us. I gradually felt some relief.

The Best of Times

From the summer of 1999 to the summer of 2002, Karla stabilized. For most of that time she stayed on her meds, received counseling, went back to school in Stillwater, and lived a relatively normal student life. During these six semesters, she maintained a GPA of 4.0. She even studied in Poland one semester, taught English to a class of Polish adults (some of whom became her friends), and visited Auschwitz. She was deeply moved by what she saw and learned there, particularly because she read and studied many memoirs of Holocaust victims and was writing a paper on her reaction to that terrifying, devastating piece of history.

During these years she also maintained healthy relationships both on a social level and a personal level. She reconnected with some high school friends—Mandy, Molly, and the entire Swiney family in particular. She had deep and wholesome friendships with Marie, Mindie, and Michelle. She also entered into a close and long lasting relationship with Art, a kind, sensitive, and intelligent English professor at OSU who shared many of her convictions and interests. Karla's friendships blossomed during these years. She connected with people of all walks of life and her genuine care for each one of them was evident.

I began to feel better along with her. The possibility of relapse always lingered in my heart and soul. But as time went on, I became more confident that the extremes of her illness were successfully and permanently contained. Karla's design in the unfolding Smith family tapestry began to take on brighter, more hopeful colors and shapes. The heavy, dreary, frightening threads of the past few years no longer dominated the texture of our family life.

My worry and concern for her drifted into issues like her coming graduation and whether she would get a masters and how she would finance her life. She seemed safe enough, although she liked living on the edge of society. We talked regularly about her future, her finances, and her relationships. None of these issues matched the intensity, fear, and confusion of the previous battles with depression and mania. Once I peeked into her empty grave, everything else was manageable.

3

Five Threads

To appreciate what was happening to Karla, and therefore to the rest of us, at this time, I need to outline five interwoven themes. These threads weave in and out of her life and our family tapestry in a way that is hard to pin down but which color all other events. The first is medication, the second is jobs, the third revolves around her self-esteem, the fourth is her spirituality, and the fifth is her writing.

The Medication Roller Coaster

I decided not to include her various medications during the narrative of her life from 1996 to the summer of 2002 in chapter 2. I simply don't know all the times, places, and changes in her medication. She had many different doctors and counselors. They all tried to prescribe a combination of meds that would help her, but there was no agreement about the various prescriptions and dosages. Each person is different, with slightly different body chemistry, and therefore what works well for one bipolar person may not work for another. Besides, an effective combination of meds may not remain as effective over time. The world of mental illness and medication is frustrating, confusing, unreliable, expensive, and, when given with a cavalier attitude, downright demeaning. It is basically trial and error, with the error having, at times, tragic consequences.

There is also no database or efficient way of sharing medical or medication history. Karla entered many mental health institutions, doctors' offices, clinics, and emergency rooms, and none of them gave any indication that they knew anything about her medical history. She couldn't tell them because she was either deeply depressed or manic at the time. We tried to inform the doctors and nurses what we knew but, in general, it was hit and miss. In the meantime, she was simply given whatever medication the current doctor thought best—or whatever was on hand. And since she moved a lot, she seldom received long-term care from a single source.

We (Fran, Kevin, and I) were convinced very early on that proper medication was a key to her mental health. We didn't know which pill she needed, except that lithium, or a lithium substitute, was critical in controlling the mania. There are many types of antidepressants, and we weren't sure which one fit her situation, but we knew she needed at least one of them. Most of the time Karla agreed—more so regarding the depression than the mania. She was always concerned about the side effects of various drugs, which could include at times, weight gain, nausea, tremors, dizziness, possible liver damage, etc. She was writing her memoirs which focused on her illness, and the operating title of one version of the manuscript was "Glue." The title referred to her medication; she believed it was the glue that held her life together.

At other times, like most bipolar victims, she resisted taking her medication. In these moods, she did not want to be dependent on pills for the rest of her life. She feared the side effects and wanted to believe that she could conquer the illness without medication, or with herbs, yoga, and other "natural" methods. Chemically, the major problem was that her body did not produce enough lithium to regulate the impulses in her brain. She needed the lithium like a diabetic needs insulin. Why she didn't produce enough lithium naturally is still unknown, and it would be extremely valuable if medical research could pinpoint that cause. More genetic research would also be helpful. Like other bipolar persons, she was attracted to the manic experience, at least in its milder forms. But for the most part, she was faithful in taking her medication, particularly from the summer of 1999 up to the summer of 2002.

Just to give you an idea what I am talking about regarding the various medications she took at different times, let me list what I know were some of her prescriptions. Like I said, I am not absolutely certain when or in what order or in what combination she took these pills, but I know she took: Lithium, Zyprexa, Zoloft, Prozac, Risperdol, Wellbrutin, Valporic Acid, Xanax, Clonopin, Paxcil, Haldol, Effexor, and Ritalin. There are probably others as well. She took some of these medications a few different times and in different combinations, depending on whatever current doctor she had and where she lived.

I always encouraged her to keep taking her pills but, at times, I didn't know what they were. I was convinced she needed them and I trusted the doctors that she had the right prescriptions in the right dosages and in the right combinations. As things ultimately turned out, I shouldn't have been so trusting. On the other hand, who am I to second-guess a psychiatrist when it comes to prescribing medication for bipolar illness?

Going to Work

Her job history is as difficult to trace as her medication history. Many college students change jobs often, but Karla went way beyond that norm. Most of the time her illness prevented her from keeping a job. When she was stable, she did relatively well. At one point she worked out of a temp agency, and she also spent a number of months at WillCom in Tulsa. There were a lot of fast-food jobs, including McDonalds and Subway, and she was a waitress at a few casual dining restaurants. One time when she was just coming out of a depressive episode, Applebee's hired her as a waitress. She lasted three or four days. Here was this lovely young woman who won prizes in speech and drama all her life, and she couldn't talk to customers well enough to take their order for lunch. It was painful, and she just couldn't do it.

She never made nearly enough money to pay any taxes, but each year we would help her when she had to file. She would have one W4 form for $88 from one place and another form for $43 from a different place.

When she was in school—that was her job, though sometimes she would try to get a paying job as well. When she couldn't go to school, her mental health was her job. But it was a delicate balance. Fran and I felt that working was also part of her therapy. Doctors and counselors often agreed. We would encourage her to get a job in order to give her something to do, and to have a reason to get out of bed, especially when she was coming off a period of depression. She certainly needed the money, but more importantly she needed to focus on something and someone other than herself in order to regain some stability. On the other hand, there were times when she simply was incapable of dealing with the responsibilities and relationships inherent in working. It was hard to tell when she was unable to work and when she needed encouragement and direction to get a job. I doubt if she knew where that fine line was. We certainly didn't, and that insecurity added more painful confusion to our stumbling efforts to love and support her.

She wasn't opposed to work, and she wasn't naturally lazy. She kept her dorms and apartments neat and clean, decorated always with her elegant style and personal signature. She lived in some pretty dreary places, but she could put her artistic touch on any living space. Cooking was a special interest and she delighted in making a pasta dinner, inviting friends, creating an atmosphere with candles and music, opening a bottle of wine, and serving a delicious meal with unique spices and a few hours of animated conversation.

She also worked hard as a student. She loved to learn and to read. Television was only useful when it had a VCR as a means to watch movies, usually thought-provoking, weighty films that demanded hours of analysis. She did watch enough "regular TV" to know about *Friends, Whose Line Is It Anyway?* (she loved those improvs!) and a few others. But she could go for months without paying much attention to television. She had her books and her music, and she got her news from National Public Radio.

I was always convinced that once she got through school and got a "real job," she would be an excellent employee. At that point, she would be committed to her profession and she would give her all. I figured she would end up an English teacher, perhaps in high school or maybe in college. She also talked about being a therapist, and if she could become stable and reliable, she would be an excellent one. I am convinced that regardless of her "day job," she would also be a published author. In fact, she wrote so well, with such insight, images, and language that writing could become her primary profession.

Between 1996 and 2002, she did not find her niche in the work world.

Folded into her job experiences was her attitude toward money. During manic episodes she didn't see the need for money and certainly not our current economic system. She figured people should simply share their needs and gifts with each other, and everyone would be okay. Barter was at the heart of her economic utopia and, unlike most of us who dream of different social or economic systems, she tried to live by her ideals and gave away money, a lot of "things," and literally the clothes off her back.

When she was depressed, money was the least of her concerns. Weightier issues weighed her down. When she was relatively stable, she accepted the need for financial security and managed her money quite well. She just didn't have enough of it to meet basic needs. We, of course, financed her through most of her schooling and illness, but we also expected her to contribute what she could to her living expenses. It was always difficult to determine just where she was on the mental health scale (except when she was obviously either very manic or clinically depressed) and so it was equally thorny trying to establish where she was money-wise and what we should do about it. Like all parents, we wanted to guide her into responsible budgeting and encourage her to become financially independent. She understood the goal, but her illness, her status as a student, and her belief that many other things were much more important than money prevented her from getting there.

Her Self-Esteem

Her self-esteem was another area that defied definition. A simple reading of her writing exposes her brittle ego. Most people either have a basic sense of self-worth or they don't. We struggle through some demanding times, usually throughout adolescence, but end up as young adults with our self-esteem pretty well established or significantly battered. In either case, most of us learn to adjust and get by in life. For Karla, the struggle for a consistent sense of self-worth was a major casualty of her illness. She could be very confident, self-assured, proud of her accomplishments, and absolutely convinced that she was a woman of many gifts, with an engaging personality and a power to persuade others to see the world as she did. She charmed many men and maintained solid relationships with many women. But when the depression began to seep into her soul, her self-esteem deteriorated rapidly. Eventually, she would be convinced that she wasn't worth the few chemicals that comprised her body and certainly not the time or energy the people who loved her would spend on her. She was a hindrance to herself, to others, and to the world in general. She did not deserve to take up space on planet Earth. She failed at everything. Her self-esteem transformed into self-loathing, shame, and guilt. And that transformation didn't take long.

Her Spiritual Search

The fourth theme also deserves mentioning at this point because it too mingles with her core reality. Even in the extremes of her depressions and her mania, she believed in God and was aware of living on a spiritual level. Her concept of God changed depending on the state of her illness. But even when she was most depressed, she didn't believe in a punishing God. She felt shame and guilt, but it was more like

God shouldn't spend time on her because she wasn't worth the attention rather than God should punish her. When she was manic, her image of God was an active part of her life, and her motivation was consistently rooted in a deep-seated and genuine desire to help create a spiritual union among people. When she was stable, her search for spiritual meaning took a number of turns, reverses, and bumpy roads, including an attraction to paranormal teachings like horoscopes and tarot cards and regular returns to her Catholic roots, but the spiritual search was always there, actively motivating, comforting, and simultaneously challenging her. To read her poetry, essays, and manuscripts is to join her on this search.

With Pen in Hand

Karla was always a superb writer. She lived in countless dorms, apartments, houses, cities, and countries. Periodically, she moved back home with us, usually after a hospitalization. She was able to move often and quickly because she had very little. She was amazingly unattached to "things." During a manic phase, she simply left things for others, including a computer we bought her, and she once gave her student loan money to a homeless man in Tulsa. Her books, a few Georgia O'Keefe posters, some small mementoes, and her writings were her only constants. She kept everything she ever wrote, including a seventh grade journal and most of her personal letters. She was a writer and expected to be published.

She wrote on many topics in many forms. Memoirs, poetry, essays, articles, books, and even her personal letters contain passages that demonstrate her insight, wisdom, sensitivity, convictions, and struggles. Her language is captivating. She thinks and writes in images, easily communicating complicated ideas and feelings with a colorful comparison, clarifying reference, or poetic prose.

Her writing began with her reading. She read constantly; her books were usually related to literature, poetry, philosophy, theology, or feminism. Novels didn't interest her much unless they were classics. She also read many memoirs of people who were bipolar in order to compare experiences and to discover her unique way of writing her own memoir.

These five dimensions—medication, jobs, self-esteem, spirituality, and writing—are essential to get a glimpse of Karla during these years. These five threads of her reality, combined with her illness, her relationships, her complex personality, her gifts, and her unique spirit combine to create the wonderful mystery, the charming and challenging young woman, the beautiful, intelligent, and engaging person I proudly and lovingly call my daughter.

4

Karla Speaks for Herself

In this chapter you meet Karla through her own written words. There are three lengthy passages. I include them not because I think they are the best examples of her best writing, but because they reveal some of her thinking, style, and perspective on her illness. Two of the three sections relate specifically to her bipolar experience, each written at a different stage during a recovery period. The other passage, and the first quote here, reflects her ongoing search for the approach she would take in writing her memoir. She was committed to telling her story but had not yet settled on the basic method she wanted to take. Given some more time, she would have clarified her perspective and produced a best seller. I am absolutely convinced of that.

"Comments on Other Memoirs and Plans for My Own"

"In all the memoirs of mental illness that I've read, each author at some point laments that it is impossible to really describe acute depression (or mania or schizophrenia); the experience itself defies words. This is discouraging. But I want this problem to be a theme of my book, directly addressed and worked through: the very impossibility of writing what I am trying to write. Similar to the experience of an acute episode itself, the causes of the illness are equally elusive. I have to remember the truth that William Styron, in his book <u>Dark-</u>

ness Visible, so plainly declares: 'I shall never learn what "caused" my depression, as no one will ever learn about their own. To be able to do so will likely forever prove to be an impossibility, so complex are the intermingled factors of abnormal chemistry, behavior and genetics.' There is no accounting for why mental illness strikes some and not others. As Styron says, 'Bloody and bowed by the outrages of life, most human beings still stagger on down the road, unscathed by real depression. To discover why some people plunge into the downward spiral of depression, one must search beyond the manifest crisis—and then still fail to come up with anything beyond wise conjecture.'

"I am so captivated by Styron's book because it combines the details of his own story with more general discussions of important questions surrounding mental illness. If this book were widely read in the '90's, as I have heard it was, then he has contributed crucial understandings to those who have never suffered from severe depression; for example, he argues that the stigma and shame commonly attached to suicide, the frequent assumption that the person must have been weak, is just ridiculous and must be replaced by a more sympathetic awareness that a person commits suicide because the psychic torment is simply too much to endure.

"Like Styron, I want to include some critical comments about the larger world, using examples from my own life as starting points. For example, I want to question the capacity of any institution to administer carefully and correctly to the patient suffering from mental illness, and instead of proposing mere reform, I'd like to envision a completely radical method of treatment (still working out the details of this in my head). I also want to situate my story within a larger sociological framework: growing up in an American, upper-middle class, religious family, with pressures to succeed, and I want to express the 'depression-inducing' elements of those circumstances (while still refusing to name a singular cause of my illness). But my story also visits the impoverished underside of society and I especially want to point out the vast difference between hospitals for the rich and for the poor. Along similar lines, I want to look at gender: I want to show

how it does, at least partially, make sense that my brother did not suffer depression but I did; how it works in adolescence that so much of a girl's self esteem is derived from her looks and attention from boys, and how hard it is to out-grow this; and, drawing largely on Showalter's amazing book The Female Malady, how frailty, dependence, and even madness have been linked with the Western conception of woman since Aristotle.

"I also want to consider religion: the Catholicism of my youth, my intellectual infatuation with Judaism (which ironically contributed to my first depression), the universalism of the New Age and Eastern mysticism that was so much a part of my mania, the 'Higher Power' practicality of AlAnon, and the atheism I have, at other times, found irresistible. A lot of my story has to do with religion and spirituality, and it is a delicate matter, because I do not want any of these ways of thinking to come out looking like the bad guy, or a cause of my problems, or the right or wrong answer to existential questions. For each, I want to make it clear why it was so appealing to me at the time, especially in the case of the New Age spiritualism of my mania, which I do not want to convey as simple madness. Somehow I want to do it justice, but as it stands now, in the sections I've written about my mania, the whole way of thinking can be written off as delusional or arrogant. I think I need a lot of guidance in my sections about mania, and about religion.

"I want to address these larger questions in my book because too many of the memoirs of mental illness I have read do not. Most such books follow a simple narrative, always in chronological order, never with any speculation outside of the narrator's own story. There is always a basic pattern: I was fine, I got sick, I got better. This simple form for the telling of the story usually accompanies a refusal to look outside of one's own sociological framework. For example, one highly acclaimed memoir, An Unquiet Mind, by Kay Redfield Jamison, is an elegant piece of writing, with the best descriptions of mania I have ever read, but the writer herself is a psychiatrist, and so she never questions the medication-hospital form of treatment. Also, she is a well educated, wealthy doctor from a rich military family, and she never addresses the issue of class, which undoubtedly determined the treatment she received, at one of the best and most expensive hospitals in the nation. Another troubling issue of her narrative is that she often lapses into long adoring descriptions of people in her life, as though she knows quite well that they will read her book. As much as possible, I want to imagine an anonymous audience. At times I catch myself editing for the sake of a parent or friend who might read a certain section, and I have to resist this temptation. Also, with the exception of a few passages about mania, I cannot help but think that Jamison remains somewhat distant and detached from what she writes. The flow of the book is, from a literary perspective, flawlessly sensible and straightforward. Her command of the language is impressive. But I want my book to resemble, even in its form and structure, the subject matter.

"The common formula and simple chronology of 'I was sick and I got better' cannot work for me, mostly because I think there are too many far more interesting alternatives, but also because it isn't entirely true: I am still a manic-depressive. Although I am on the right medication and I basically function and I do not lose everything in major episodes anymore, I am not 'cured.' I fight the depressive tendencies all the time. I don't know how to integrate that into my story, but I know it needs to be there, if I am to write an honest book. Even the best of all mental illness memoirs, Sylvia Plath's The Bell Jar, ends on an inspiring note: a kind of 'fixing of the problem' (which is sadly ironic, in light of what we now know of her suicide). William Styron ends his memoir with an ultimately uplifting message, that he and many others have gotten out of the depression, but he qualifies his hope with the truthful admission that many others end in suicide, and that there is no way of judging which treatments will work for an individual person (what heals one person does not heal another). So I want to avoid casting my story entirely into the past; I want to include the trouble of living with mild depression and mania, and the constant fear of another episode.

"As for the structure or form of my memoir, I basically want to experiment. As I have said, I do not want to present my life in a straight chronology; instead, I want to mention things without explaining, and then return to them again and again, so that by the end of the book, the issue or event is fully clear. I even want parts to be disorienting, confusing, but laced with clues that will make sense later. I see no better way to handle the mania, especially. I will need a lot of help ordering the sections so that they produce this unfolding effect, so there is just enough information given at the time, but not too much. Kathy Acker is my role model for structure. Her books defy all 'masculine' plot lines; sometimes the reader is utterly confused (how did she get from here to there?). However, I don't want to take it quite as far as she does. I do want an understandable narrative to emerge from my pages in the end, if convoluted in the process. The reason for this circular or disjointed structure is that I want the book to read as a real mind thinks, in brief images, triggered memories, disconnected ruminations, jumps from past to present to future, etc. Again, I will need help to know which experiments are working and which aren't.

"Something that keeps disturbing my narrative, but contributes to a less traditional structure, is that there are times when I step outside the narrative and commentary, and write about the process of writing itself. It has happened before of its own accord, when I am frustrated with the writing, or when I have just written a section as though it explains everything, and I want to insist that it is only one interpretation. I am inclined to think I want those frustrations to be a part of the book as well. At the heart of this desire to write about writing is my interest in memory, in how a sane mind can recreate the thoughts of madness that consumed it previously. Writing about writing also ties in with the present moment, living as a manic-depressive not in the throes of the illness, but always questioning past and present, gauging, trying to understand myself. I am interested in what writing one's life can do, quite literally; that is, does writing the story exile illness safely to the past, or does it trigger the illness? And I think such questions might interest my reader as well.

"Another technique I have considered using is to write some sections in other voices, first person from the perspective of a family member, or friend, or staff person at the hospital. Since reading <u>The Quiet Room</u>, by Lori Schiller and Amanda Bennet, I am hesitant to try this because of the problems it easily causes. They (Schiller is schizophrenic; Bennet is her ghost writer) include sections 'by' her mother, father, brothers, and a therapist, but they don't work because there is no tension between these sections and those in first person by the main character. For the technique to work the reader must learn something new from the sections 'by' other people; they cannot simply reinforce what the primary voice says about the other person. It would be tricky, but I will experiment with it.

"Susanna Kaysen, in <u>Girl, Interrupted</u> experiments with the form of her memoir. For example, she includes actual photocopies of medical records and notes by doctors, interspersed with her own voice (the contrast between the psychiatric jargon and her more poetic confusion is telling, and effective). In fact, I want to obtain my own records to use similarly in my book, but no hospital will release them to me without the intervention of a lawyer (still working on this). A few short chapters in Kaysen's book use other creative devices, such as 'Etiology,' which is a multiple choice test offering interpretations of why she is going mad, and another, less effective chapter is a direct quote from the DSM IV (the 'bible' of psychiatric disorders) on her diagnosis, Borderline Personality Disorder. But even with these innovative devices, much of her book reads like a novel in which various strange personalities interact on the psych ward. Again, like Jamison but in a different way, Kaysen is detached from the experience she tries to relate; or maybe, unlike me, she is more interested in describing the outer experience of hospital life than her internal world. Another sign that she remains detached from her inner experience is that the tone of the book is almost always ironic, sarcastic, attempting humor and levity. I want some of a similar tone in parts of my book, but I certainly won't use it throughout.

One extremely important book I read, <u>Beyond Bedlam,</u> is a compilation of short vignettes by women who have been hospitalized for mental illness in recent decades. The book is so important because of its critical edge; it is essentially a feminist and progressive analysis of the current hospital experience. Most of the writers are by no means professional, but some use an appealing humor, which is at times morbid and usually ironic, when they talk about the inane staff or procedures in such places. In reading writers who are actually more like myself, in their inexperience with writing, than literary geniuses like Styron, Acker, or Plath, I took a few hints; for example, I must avoid certain over-used banalities in metaphors of depression and mania (a dark cloud, a maze, a shadow, a wall, tears of pain, etc.). This book is also important to me because it inspires me to continue writing my memoir; it reassures me when I am in doubt, when I think it's not worthwhile to write this book. It affirms that we who have suffered at the hands of the disease and the hospitals must tell our own stories, or others will tell them, untruthfully. But I often do have reservations about writing this memoir. I would like to discuss this with you when I come home."

To Whom It May Concern

The next passage was written during her stable years of 2000 and 2001 and, as best as I can determine, before the section you just read. She had completed seven chapters of a proposed eleven chapter book initially titled *To Whom It May Concern, A Personal Letter to the Chosen Suffering from Depression*. It is not a final draft and ultimately this manuscript would probably become part of her book titled *Glue* or perhaps folded into a book that was not yet titled. In any case, these excerpts introduce you to the strong Karla, the Karla who felt confident enough to try to map the experience of depression and to offer suggestions to other depression victims on how to combat this destructive illness.

"You must rise from the ashes. You have no choice. You no longer have the luxury of lying about, thinking of death and escape, ignoring everyone who loves you. It is not an option anymore.

"The one concept at the heart of what I must tell you is this. There is only one place in the world where the most sacred, beautiful, and mighty treasure lies, and that is the place where you stand. I say: drink that, shout that, for everything points to it.

"You disagree. It's obvious you have not been treated as sacred, and there are so many people more beautiful than you, and you feel as mighty as a flea. The misery is like swallowing knives, or else it is an apathy that even watching your life crumble all about you cannot budge. It's nearly impossible to think of this treasure you supposedly are when nothing would seem better than slipping off into oblivion. Hard as you might try to self-medicate, the drinking and drugs and sleeping only leave you waking to an even lower self esteem. Or perhaps it is the routine of holding up appearances that you are a success after all, that the kids are taken care of, and you have a spotless attendance record at work, and is this all there is? You doubt that other people are as alone as you are, despite the bustle of activity you are able to maintain. You doubt that you have done it right, that you could ever get the hang of this life, complete with normal ups and downs that are to be expected. You doubt that the whole world was made for only you. Such notions are pretty, perhaps tempting, but with the weathered, hardened feel in your heart, a simple impossibility to embrace. I say that you have not done it all wrong, that you have not missed the boat, or gotten yourself into a fix that might take years to unravel. I say that your thinking problems amount to one thing: you are not grateful.

"Gratitude is your way out of this. Henri Nouwen wrote a book called the <u>Return of the Prodigal Son</u>, in which he points out an important part in the story most people overlook. Typically, the younger son is seen as the guilty one, forsaking his roots and wandering aimlessly, wasting what has been given him. Yes, he does have little awareness of what matters in life until he embraces his father. But before those of you who have not led reckless lives pass this story by, notice the elder son. He insists that he deserves a celebration from the father, for he has stayed by his side, done what is honorable, and certainly should win his father's sole favor. Essentially, he is consumed by resentment and jealousy. He thinks he has done no wrong.

"Haven't we all felt cheated out of what 'should be' ours? Did we demand that life feed us the gravy, for we have been so miraculously unerring? We lose sight of the fact that life itself does not owe us anything. We assume that we enter the world deserving a checklist of things that would make our emotional journey easier. From a societal standpoint, we do deserve certain rights of freedom and expression, but no one could ever guarantee that we would also have happiness. We mistakenly think that we must receive this advantage or that relationship to fulfill us. Don't you think that if we had our every wish granted, were given everything we say would make us happy, we would only proceed to compile a new list of wants, and the wanting would be endless? What we do have full possession of is the inherent capacity for happiness. I assure you, that capacity is already overflowing with blessings that we do not yet know how to call blessings. Every person, circumstance or gift you have received which lends itself to the fullness and enjoyment of your life is, then, a blessing, and not something to take for granted.

"It might not be obvious that certain people or situations in your life are blessings, and to this I reply that we do not always know the reason for what happens in our lives. Often we throw our arms up in the air wondering why we have to deal with him or her, or why there isn't enough money this month, or why we were laid off, but it is only that we are not yet able to see the whole picture. It will be revealed for us as time goes on, if we are watching for it. Meanwhile, even without being able to see the reasons for what is happening, we are able to choose what approach to take to it all. Everything, absolutely everything, can be viewed in both a positive and a negative light.

"Be grateful whether you think things are going well or not. Gratitude will liberate you from the prison of wanting more in your life. I read a book once which said, 'Happiness is not found in seeking more, but in developing the capacity to enjoy less.' The elder son in our story has his father's affection all the time, but wants more, wants the affection his brother receives as well. How much gratitude does the elder son have for all his blessings? None. Which is why he also has no joy.

"So without gratitude, you will continually bang your head on the wall of resentment. If you must lie in your bed much of the time (and the amazing thing is that you don't have to, as it might seem), lie there and count your blessings. Which, I know, is a tall order. But you will have to attempt, with all your might, to focus on what there is to hold dear, instead of your usual litany of resentments. Make your mental list of what there is to rejoice in, and repeat it to yourself throughout the day, whatever you may be doing. The list is endless. Haven't you arms that move, and toes that wiggle in the bath, and a heart that feeds blood throughout your body? You are not without a mind, and although it is fogged, it can choose what your body will do next. You have eyes that show you the majesty of a sunrise, the hopping of a bird, the trembling of a leaf, the grin of a child. Do these things seem insignificant? Mushy? Like a Halmark card? Then you are not truly looking. For everywhere, there are hidden and striking scenes which speak a message through your wall of rose thorns that separates you from the world.

"For example, there is a certain bird that makes a call into the summer night, much like the questioning hoot of the owl. When I was depressed, I would sit out on the back porch with tea and cigarettes, forcing myself to think of nothing but that eerie, mellow bird call, and for small moments at the time, I was content. It's no long-term solution, but when you are suffering, even temporary distractions offer some morsel of relief. As hard as it may seem, splash some water on your face, find a small place for only you. Try to still your thoughts by focusing on some curious sound or sight outside yourself. Then make it a habit. Each day, treat yourself to this release, and perhaps you will find a regular respite from the nearly continuous treadmill of thinking.

"Also think of the people in your life. They, too, are blessings. But he screams at me, you say, they whine and misbehave, she doesn't even look my way. You have long-standing destructive relationships with people in your life, in both subtle and screaming ways. You feel there is little you can do about this, for the patterns were established long ago. But although so many people are enormously faulted creatures, and being entangled with them often leads to recurring habits of self destruction and mutual sick dependency, they are only human and not much more can be expected of them. They have faults, just like you do. Couched within their shortcomings lies their beauty; it is often the case that one's faults are simply their good points taken to extremes. You have no option but to learn how to protect yourself in the midst of people who possess varying amounts of sickness; you must learn to distinguish you from them and proceed in the relationships, somehow keeping yourself safe. Would you prefer a world with no fault? Some would answer yes. But what would be the point of us being here? With nothing to learn from each other? Think of a world with no free will, a factory run by robots, who do not cry out or demand. They do not carry around an amazing burden of fears which prompt them to treat you in frightening ways. And then think of having a child and caring only that she be fed, have her diapers changed, and be kept from dangerous situations. Your only concern is that she continues to live, for this is how a robot looks after a child. Is it not infinitely more earth shattering that we feel, explode, crave, rejoice? Do we not nearly burst with love for that child? If you want to dispense with the fear and the anger, you must also get rid of the beauty. Do not wonder at the fact that there is suffering in your life at the hands of other people. Wonder instead that you were given so much ability to feel, to celebrate, to learn with them.

"You can also be grateful for your depression. Your suffering is the burden of most of humanity, the road the lucky travel. How could we be lucky, when the unafflicted around us appear able to juggle so many aspects of life and still have the strength to coach little league, or lead the PTA, or achieve a 3.8 GPA? Why are we lucky, when it is you and I who spend time curled up on the floor of the shower, wishing we never had to turn the water off and look at ourselves in the mirror and face the rest of the world? Where is the luck in hurting so bad, in being able to explain so little?

"There are people who wander the world without ever thinking about it, as you know. They settle in nicely, make themselves comfortable, and flip past the stations of life they do not want to watch. They might never feel hell nipping them at their heels, and they might never cry out 'why?' to a God that may or may not be there. They might perfect a million things, yet never struggle along the way. You envy them, but I tell you, it is you who are lucky, for your depression has a deep meaning and purpose. All pain serves a purpose, and its purpose is not to drive one to the overdose or the gunshot, but instead exists to teach and deepen the soul. If you feel you are learning now what there is to die for, you will someday be able to proclaim what there is to live for. The best of things come from struggle, which is not to say that it is noble to plan a life of self imposing suffering, but rather that there will inevitably be pain in your life, and this pain serves a purpose. There is a story in Scripture about Jacob wrestling with the angel at the bank of the Jordan River. There, the man was made lame, and received the name Israel. He emerged from the encounter blessed and prepared to live within the will of the Lord. You are wrestling with the angel, and there is much you must learn from him before you are released. Never lose sight of the fact that this is a spiritual battle, perhaps unlike what your psychologists call it, but I assure you, it is your spirit and soul that must be freed. Why is it so essential that you fight? Because there is too much at stake to not fight. Because there is only one place in the world where the greatest treasure lies, and that is where you stand.

"There are two kinds of people when it comes to depression: those who understand and those who don't. You can easily tell who's who. Find one who does understand, and listen. Let them love you until you are able to love yourself. You may be having a mental Ping-Pong match with these people. They offer a suggestion or word of hope, and you bat it back to them tarnished and nearly broken. You have a rebuttal for every possible good idea that comes your way. What do you benefit from this? You nestle yourself more firmly into your briar patch, all for the sake of wanting to sound more knowing. You must be open to new ways of thinking, because it was not the circumstances in your life that got you where you are now, but your own thinking. Listen to the teachers in your life, and allow them to proceed on their journey to God by helping you.

"I am grateful to find teachers not only in the people in my life who know something about meaning, but also in the poetry I read and the music I listen to. A musical group sings the lyrics, 'What made me think I could start clean slated? The hardest to learn was the least complicated,' which means that the answers are simple. I had to learn that there was not some evasive equation that held the secret, forever escaping my understanding. You do not need to start clean slated to understand what you have known all along. You must return to whence you came, rekindle wonder at the miracles around you. We were born in God's image, faulted, yes, but nonetheless we remain inherently good, and we cannot shake the vein of light from our souls. No matter what you have done, you have not reversed your nature. Stop fearing that you are bad, less than, inadequate, because at your birth you were made holy. Try as you might, your inherent good nature does not change. You were given the answers then and have only covered and clouded them with fear. Try for one day to live as a child does, and you will see for yourself the goodness remaining within you.

"I am requesting what to you must sound like a directive to sprout wings and fly to the moon. Think as a child, stop fearing you are bad. What good does this do when you are so used to your negativity that such statements sound like a joke? I agree, they might sound impossible at first, which is why you cannot only think of such ideas once, as you read this. You must get used to the sound of them. Repeat them to yourself. Much good can come from mantras, silly as they may seem. Since your mind is a virtual wasteland of unfocused ideas, since they all seem to point in the direction of hopelessness, think of the relief there might be in replaying over and over some words of hope. When you are depressed, certain thought patterns take possession of your mind and burrow their way along pathways, engraining themselves into you. It is almost like getting a song stuck in your head, hour after hour. You can do the same with positive thoughts.

"But you don't believe the pep talks; you can't say the cute little optimistic phrases with any sincerity. It doesn't matter if you believe yet what you say. The mind does not know the difference between thinking of reality and thinking in make believe. Say them even though they might appear to be the most ridiculous notions in your present state. The God's honest truth is that they are not. And you become what you think. I'm going to make it out of this hell, I'm going to make it out, I'm going to make it, I am …

"I am grateful for people, music, and also history and literature. Here you see that you do not suffer alone. 'What comfort is that?' I asked in my dark days. It is the knowledge that all is connected, many have wrestled, and many have overcome. The mindset you are in leaves you breathlessly alone, shockingly isolated, but it is only a myth that there are no role models here, no soldiers who fought and lived.

"Poetry, music, literature, and history all teach us something about ourselves, and there is another surprising teacher to be grateful for. When I was severely depressed, I met with Susan, my therapist, twice a week. At the lowest of my days, much of my time with her consisted of silence, not through any fault of hers, but because I could not speak. My eyes darted around the room, mostly on the floor, often on the merciless clock that kept me strapped to my chair. She would wait, and then ask, 'Are your thoughts racing so fast you can't get them out, or is your mind a blank?' And I didn't know even that. I

thought that our silence was nearly impossible to bear, as well as ridiculous, as well as costly. I thought, 'I can do this at home. It's my
career, after all, to sit and stare at things.' Recently, however, I have
read something which points to how important that time with her
was. Elie Wiesel, in <u>Dawn</u>, says that 'the silence between two people is
deeper than the silence of one.' This means that though nothing is
said, much can be conveyed. The fact that the other person is there,
choosing to be with you, is a testimony to the sort of love that is possible for you now, even at your darkest moments. When two people
share a silence, a presence of the Between is established with them,
and be it that the intentions of the two people are in harmony and for
each other, the Between is synonymous with the Above. Meaning that
God is present, and the silence is Him.

"So perhaps you spend most of your time alone, thinking endlessly, and trapping yourself in those thoughts. Most likely there are
people who are concerned for you, and stand by helplessly as you
grow more and more isolated. You are tired of their trite pick-me-ups,
and hollow suggestions, and sugary anecdotes. They ask what they
can do to help, and they offer words that do not penetrate your thick
cloud. Tell one of these friends that you do not really want to talk,
but that it would help you to be with him or her, perhaps to read in
the same room, or do some cooking, or watch a movie. Maybe you
need to get out of your usual environment, so ask if you could come
over and spend some time doing your own thing at their house. The
end of the day will be different than the end of most days. You can say
to yourself that you did something today; you shared something
sacred with a friend.

"You might be saying to yourself now that you do have every reason to be depressed because you do not have such a friend that cares
and would like to spend some time with you. But there are things you
can do to achieve the same sense of connectedness, if you are willing
to look at togetherness a little differently than you usually do. You
could take a walk where people are, or go to a playground where children play, or even become a volunteer to get yourself in touch with

other people. While you are there, you can think of all the things you know you have in common with them, without ever speaking of these shared feelings. Certainly, they hurt at times too; they need, and love, and feel regret and most everything that you yourself feel, just perhaps not with the same intensity. The idea here is to show yourself that you are not alone, you are not unique. A friend in AlAnon put it to me this way when I was depressed: 'You are not half as important as you think you are, but you are much more important than you ever thought you could be.'

"And here I am telling you what to do. Knowing full well that that's what everyone does, and it's usually pointless, not to mention insulting. I told my friend Judith that I was writing this book and she wrote to me, unconvinced that I was undertaking a project that would have much effect. She wrote, 'Remember when I used to come round to see you when you were really depressed and I always felt like I ought to have some sort of solution for things, and to argue against you when you said something negative? How much of a difference did it make to you for me to say those things?' And she is right, most of what she said when I was depressed fell on deaf ears. Just like much of this might be futile in its attempt to help anyone. But that is a chance I have to take. What is my alternative? To stay silent and not respond to what I have learned through my own experience is to not have learned those lessons at all."

Another Version

A year or so after Karla wrote those words for people who suffer from depression, she took a little different approach. She certainly didn't disavow herself of this text, and its message remains valid and helpful. She simply explored another way to deal with her experience and how she wanted to share it with others.

In early July 2002, she joined us in Milwaukee for her cousin Mickey's wedding. It was a gala, wonderful event, surrounded by some delightful days of visiting relatives. Karla finished writing the introduction to her revised but unfinished memoir while she was in Milwaukee and distributed copies to the family. Here are her own words describing her life as she saw it at that time:

"I got better three years ago. I was ill before that. I'm still experimental and odd, searching and intense, but who I am is not squashed by and filtered through episodes of mania and depression any more. I take medication, thankfully a low dosage now, and I still feel the slight pull of mild mania or mild depression sometimes. But I take care of myself: I force myself to go to sleep when I hear my mind flirting with mania, and I force myself to start a creative project when I feel myself pulled like a magnet to lie in bed for the afternoon. I make sure I surround myself with people I love, people who will listen, who will talk me through it, who will hold me. My triggers for manic and depressive episodes are high stress, isolation, and thinking too much about me, and I am careful.

"There was a time when I was completely and utterly convinced that there was no reason for me to keep breathing. Being in my skin was painful. Every time I woke from sleeping I was crushed by the weight of my own consciousness. I lay in my bed for months at a time, not eating, not showering, not speaking to anyone. There were three major depressive episodes. They came in between attempts to do something with my life, and I really did enjoy college, I loved learning, I loved my friendships … but the depressions would hit, and within a month I'd be failing classes, terrified of friends, unable to hold a job, and back home to Broken Arrow, OK, to live with my parents.

"My parents were very supportive, in their own ways. Perhaps I wanted something more or different from them. At certain times I was convinced that they and my brother caused all my problems in the first place. Of course, they didn't. They are good people, who love me, and I was looking for somewhere to place blame. I don't look for that anymore, because no amount of self-reflection can bring me such answers. The cacophony of influences that contribute to the formation of identity is vague and mysterious. When I was depressed or manic, each member of my family had their theories about what had ruined me, and about what should be done for me to get better. I resented all of their suggestions. The only thing that was obvious to all four of us during the depressions was that I had a serious chemical imbalance, and needed medication.

"My manic episode was not so easily agreed upon; I was the dissenting member of the family meetings. I did not believe there was anything 'wrong' with me when I was manic, though afterward I began, painfully, to recognize the end of the episode as psychotic, delusional, and paranoid. The manic episode took place between the second and third depressions, and it lasted four months. In the beginning, it was wonderful. I thought I knew everything that was important to know, I thought I sensed all things, all motivations and souls of people, all movements of the Spirit through the earth, through minds, and inner planes. I had an energy that, superficially, made me 'frenetic, bossy, inexhaustible, rude, incomprehensible, according to the people who watched me go through it. I do remember how I was, and I can understand why I was described that way. But that rudeness is not the kind of energy that I really remember. I remember myself being completely in touch. In touch with what … with God, with life, with the earth, the sun, my soul, all souls, ancient feminine power, the human condition itself … it is impossible to explain, impossible, because the experience itself had nothing to do with language. The only words I can think to describe it now are words that have become so flimsy and overused that they seem to indicate different things than what I mean to say. Talking about what mania is like requires important decisions. The language a person uses to define the experience of mania says a lot about her beliefs and how she sees the world. And I haven't made up my mind yet about how to understand it.

"Or rather, I think several discourses are all true at once. I could write that my Kundalini was through the roof, expanded through my crown chakra, and that the Kriya Yoga initiation I had received lit my flame and dissolved my ego. I believe this is true. I could write that my self-esteem over the years had just worn so thin that it snapped, and I threw a sense of pride and identity to the wind (that is, I surrendered it all finally to the memories of ex-boyfriends), and said the hell with it all until I was the wild child on a fast train away from myself. I believe this is true. I could also write that I have a chemical imbalance, and this is true. But what came first, the chicken or the egg? Would this chemical imbalance have manifested if my personality from the start were different, calmer, more content to live a quiet life? Did I bring it on? Or try the story this way: I've been raised to have good Catholic values. I simply rebelled, had a prolonged adolescence, and the tricks of rebellion proved to be far more dangerous to my soul than I ever thought they could be. And this: I was 'deeply in love' from age 15 to 19, engaged to the man I loved, wrote him letters every day like a kind of diary (he went to college in Colorado). I thought I was looking at the rest of my life in photographs of him and late night phone conversations and whirlwind weekend visits. He graduated college when I finished my freshman year of college in San Antonio, and he was planning to move there, had a job lined up, and then he would marry me. We discussed it in greater detail during a trip to Europe the summer after his graduation, and we broke up in Paris. Broke my heart.

"Another story is also true: I think too much. I always have, and it's like I can't help it. It's why, when I am healthy, I delve into reading and writing; philosophy, theology, history, literature. And thinking a lot is not thinking 'too much' if the subject of thought is not me, and if I am not depressed. When I get depressed I turn all my analytical power around onto myself, judging, condemning, constructing arguments, putting on trial the people I have been in the past. I am grateful for the gifts that make me perceptive and understanding. But these gifts, filtered through the dark lenses of depression and self-loathing, can cripple me. It is impossible for me to stop thinking about me when I am depressed. And I can be merciless. As for the mania, I am naturally curious, excitable and animated, and naturally in touch to a certain extent. Mania is this nature ten thousand fold, spinning out of control.

"So these are the stories of my life. These are attempts to understand why it all happened. They are perhaps melodramatic; they are certainly too neatly and clearly stated; and they are potentially dangerous to my present tense. To write one story line, one thread through the tapestry of my past is to nudge myself toward a continuation of that story line. As I write this memoir, I want to remind myself that a new creature unfolds within me every day. Every day is an opportunity to become new, to inhabit dimensions of myself that are less familiar to me than are the stories I tell about who I am.

"I am writing to explain, to return the illness to the past, to bring the lessons of the illness into my present, to clarify what happened and why, to honor who I was and who I am becoming. I write to write the shame out of my body and mind. I write to myself, because all I have is a jumble of images, painful memories, a longing to be 'manic' again, and confusion about certain segments of time. I write to everyone in my life that watched up close, my parents, brother, and best friends, and I write to the many who love me that watched from afar, not knowing the half of it."

5

Paradise Point 2002

The progress that Karla made through 2000 and 2001 returned the Smith family to a relatively normal life. Our family tapestry was unfolding with pleasant colors and separate but interwoven designs. Kevin continued his successful career with Accenture working on projects in Richmond, Minneapolis, Chicago, and briefly in St. Louis, his home office. Fran adjusted to her role as principal of Queen of Peace Catholic elementary school, got to know the faculty, the three hundred students, and parents. I became involved with a number of exciting projects in our office, and after my boss, Irene Dill, died unexpectedly, I ultimately became the Director of Pastoral Services. Karla progressed through her junior and most of her senior year at Oklahoma State University in Stillwater. Normal enough for a family moving into the third millennium, despite the previous years of battling bipolar illness.

In November of 2001, my mother died. She was a great mom, with a gigantic, kind heart, an inquisitive mind, and values that were better than traditional because they were always renewed, personalized, and current. She was ninety-two when she finally died. All the horror stories they tell you about Alzheimer's are true. It gradually stole her fine mind and alert spirit and replaced it with a blank stare and a shrinking body. We mourned her death for seven years before we actually buried her.

After my dad died in 1984, my mom joined us for our annual family vacations. For the next eight years, mom would travel with the four of us to places like San Diego, Orlando, Sedona, Az., Massanutten Va. (visited D.C.), and Ft. Myers, Fl. Since we were the only members of her family who lived out of town, it was a cherished, yearly chance for us to be with her exclusively for a whole week. It's the way she and the twins got to know and love one another. Along with all the family activities, sights, and adventures, mom played a lot of Kismet with the kids, particularly on the one night each vacation when she insisted on babysitting while Fran and I went out on a date. Family vacations with grandma generated indelible memories and nourished relationships that live beyond the grave.

It was fitting, then, that after her funeral, we would use our small inheritance money for a Smith family vacation in her memory. But it was complicated— the twins were twenty five. Kevin was working on an out-of-town project that made it difficult to schedule a vacation when the rest of us were available. Fran and Karla couldn't get away unless it was summer. Karla also had some summer school commitments that had to be considered.

Everyone liked the idea of taking a cruise in honor of mom and, after multiple phone calls, rearrangements, meetings, and possibilities, we settled on a week and an itinerary. As it turned out, our cruise on Royal Caribbean's *Explorer of the Seas* included a stop in St. Thomas. My only specific request for the entire cruise was a family visit to Paradise Point. I was eager to be there with Karla, particularly after all the pain of the past years. I was hoping that Paradise Point would be the exclamation point on her recovery and that the peace I felt there just one year prior would seep into her as well. I knew that Kevin, too, would enjoy it, but Karla was always sensitive to the feelings of a place. To her, it was location-speak. I figured that if anyone was going to experience Paradise Point somewhat like I did, it would be Karla, especially since the major battles with bipolar disorder seemed behind us.

The cruise itself was wonderful; it gave the four of us a relaxed opportunity to be together for an extended period of time. During the days, we did some activities together, some apart, usually divided between us old folks and the twins. But every evening we got together for the consistently exquisite on-board dining followed by a show. Our dinner table included Kyle and Kelly Kocerha, a delightful honeymoon couple just a little younger than Kevin and Karla. It was animated and joyful conversation served with your choice of lobster tail, rack of lamb, peppercorn steak, and five desserts.

St. Thomas was once again toward the end of the cruise. The night before we docked I reminded the family of our plan to meet at the sky-tram at 2:00 p.m. for our lift to Paradise Point. I didn't prep them too much about my reaction the previous summer, other than to insist that it was important to me that we do this. Fran and I took a brief tour in the morning, ate on-board, shopped a little, and headed for the sky-tram at 1:45. On our way, we met Karla who was with Justin (not his real name). Justin was a young man she met on-board, a "kindred spirit," and with whom she was spending more and more time. Kevin arrived a few minutes before 2:00 and together we boarded the sky-tram to the top of Flagg Hill.

I was disappointed. I wanted this experience to be family. I met Justin briefly the day before: he seemed quiet and nice, but remote. I was concerned that Karla was getting into a cruise-relationship that would complicate her life too much. When she brought him along for our visit to Paradise Point, I was more irritated than I let on. I couldn't "forbid" his joining us but I was afraid his presence would distract Karla, and the rest of us, from the crucial Paradise Point experience I had anticipated.

I was right. Everyone enjoyed the view, drank appropriate frozen concoctions, shopped a little, and returned to the ship feeling great about the day. I still had my personal "connection" and the peace of the place touched me again. But not as deeply as the year before. Karla was distracted both by Justin and by her own lack of usual concentration. She looked beautiful in her blue sleeveless shirt, olive green shorts, with her long, blond hair pulled into a ponytail. In the pictures that Kevin took, her smile is natural, lovely, and satisfied. But her attention was not fully devoted to the setting, as I had hoped. Kevin left with his mom in order to take her to Magen's Bay before we sailed. Karla, Justin, and I remained on Paradise Point a little longer, but the "experience" never happened.

When the cruise inevitably ended, we agreed that it was a perfect way to remember my mom. We said a prayer of thanksgiving for her, to her, and with her, and flew to different destinations: Kevin to St. Louis, Fran and I to Belleville, Illinois, across the river from St. Louis, and Karla to Oklahoma State University in Stillwater.

Life had been relatively normal for a few years in our family, and our vacation together reflected this pleasant change. Just as we were comfortably settling back into our respective cities, Karla's bipolar disorder had other ideas. The illness just never goes away. Within days of our return, we knew something was terribly wrong in Stillwater. After three years of steady progress, there were signs of the beginnings of another major attack of mania and depression. Karla's telephone conversations were scattered, somewhat incoherent, and her energy level was boundless. Her friends, Art and Marie, reported similar behavior. All the raw memories of her manic episode in 1998 flashed ominously through my startled soul. The immediate future loomed like dark, rampaging, deadly Oklahoma clouds spitting out multiple, fierce tornadoes. I was terrified.

6

My Sister
July 29–August 15, 2002

In the days and weeks following the cruise, Karla's growing mania destroyed our normal way of reacting to her and to daily events in general. The mania made it impossible to keep up with her or even to remember yesterday's events. It reached proportions unparalleled to her previous episode. It took so much concentration to respond to the immediate, present moment that there was little energy or ability to put today's experience into any ongoing context. Our family tapestry was unraveling.

As the mania began to threaten Karla's safety and general well-being, Kevin became even more concerned. He recorded his involvement in the chronology that follows. This chronology served two purposes. The first and obvious aim was to maintain a clear record of the people, places, and events swirling around Karla so all of us could help her better. The second purpose was personal: Kevin wanted to show Karla later how the mania affected him, and what he did to support and love her. He hoped, at the end of this manic episode, reading his chronology would help her avoid this situation in the future. This chapter of *The Tattered Tapestry* is the first part of his chronology.

Chronology of Events

Week of July 29, 2002

- Unknown to everyone, Karla has stopped taking her medicine. Suspected date she stopped was around July 1. Likely phased out dosage gradually.

- Karla has an incident at her job, where she does home visits with mentally challenged adults. She claims her patient, Ron, verbally assaulted her. Rob Barnes, her supervisor, has trouble believing the extent of the attack. Karla is told to take a leave of absence from work and that she will never be assigned to Ron again. It is my presumption that this was the beginning of her major manic stage, and past experiences gave her the impression that the alleged attack with Ron was much more severe than it actually was. Her thoughts are becoming unclear.

- Karla travels to Tulsa to stay with a good friend, Lonnie, for a few days. Lonnie is a man in his early 40s who also suffers from periodic depression. They met a few years back at Perry's restaurant in Tulsa. Lonnie lives in an apartment in his father's vending machine warehouse. He has a deep spirituality, insight, and affection for Karla. Her manic warning signs are beginning.

- We speak briefly on July 31, and Karla explains to me that her patient at work in Stillwater assaulted her, and she needed to go to Tulsa to be with people who understood her. Says she will call back to tell me the full story. She never calls back.

- Aug. 2: 3:00 a.m.—Karla leaves a message on my cell phone telling me that I am the best brother, everything is fine, and she appreciates all my support. Certainly a sign of the mania, which is starting to become more apparent.

Wednesday Morning, August 7–Our Birthday

- 10:00 a.m.–11:00 a.m.—I call Karla to wish her a Happy Birthday.

- Karla is in an extreme manic episode. Listens to nothing that I say. Repeatedly tells me that she has found the spiritual divine through meditation.

- Explains that she has gone on a spiritual journey this past week with five other people: Lonnie, Mandy Hayes, Justin (met on cruise), Dr. Patterson (former professor), and Elie Wiesel, the Jewish holocaust survivor, author, and spokesman. These people have connected through recent news events and have special powers throughout the world. Karla is their spiritual guide and now understands everything about their cause.

- Karla has now been called through divine intervention to lead the Spiritual Convention Center in Tulsa. Mandy will be operating it with her. Karla has spoken with several priests who support her cause and will help her financially.

- Explains that she will now be separated from Art, her former fiancé, because it is what is meant to be. He has met another woman in Belarus. Karla has plans to move back to Tulsa and talks about living forever with her soul mate, Justin.

- Karla invites me to a birthday party she is having tonight with her friends in Stillwater. Remember, it is now 11:00 a.m. and I am in St. Louis. She said she would understand if I can't come, but will also invite dad (also currently in the St. Louis area). Several priests from the area are also invited, and Karla is convinced they will attend. Karla plans to cook a large meal and feed everyone. She has been called by the spirit to do so. (She never does cook the meal, but provides some burritos for her guests.)

- I tell Karla that I think she is going through a manic episode and she needs to be on her medication. She agrees. She explains that she stopped taking her medicine a few weeks ago as part of her grand plan. Now that it is her birthday, she intends to start taking the medicine again and continue to write her book. She explains that she had to experience a manic episode in order to give her the ideas and feelings she needs to complete her life story. Karla agrees that she will go see her doctor tomorrow to start taking the medication again.

- I am extremely concerned, but I do not convey this to Karla. She has gone down this path before and it is eerily similar to me. She has lost all ability to listen and reason. I saw Karla just seventeen days earlier; it is mind-boggling how her thought processes changed. She is not the same person.

- I ask to talk to Art. I want to ask him about the validity of Karla's claims and ask how he is handling this.

- Art expresses deep concern and feels helpless. He confirms her only claim that he has indeed met another woman, and Karla and he intend to separate. There appears to be little animosity about this at the moment, and Art only has genuine concern for how to help Karla. He refutes all other claims that Karla told me as untrue, namely in regard to Karla's recent spiritual journey. He does not know what she did on this weeklong journey. He is shocked by some of the thoughts and random ideas Karla has discussed during the past twenty-four hours. Her mania has gotten worse by the hour it seems. He says she has slept very little. Art did not know Karla during her first manic episode nearly four years ago, and seeing her in this state is a completely new experience. He is willing and ready to help any way that he can during this time.

- Art and I discuss the importance of Karla getting to the doctor and returning to her medication. He explains that Karla found two Effexor pills in the house. She has no other pills. She took one earlier this morning, which made her nauseated. Art agrees to make sure Karla sees her doctor on Thursday at the Oklahoma State Student Health Center.

- I explain to Art some of the behaviors Karla will likely exhibit in the next twenty-four hours as she continues to remain in her manic phase—all-knowing attitude, acting on random ideas, long breathless stories, uncontrollable laughter at times, a special spiritual relation to world events, a deep urge to analyze each individual telling them how to change their lives, and a belligerence and defiance if confronted by anyone who disagrees with her or tries to help her.

- I give Art my cell phone number and ask him to call at any time if Karla's condition worsens. I feel so much more confidence knowing that Art is involved with this situation. He is an extremely intelligent, rational man who will sacrifice anything to help and protect Karla. He's in a truly difficult situation and though I'm worried, I think everything will be okay.

Wednesday Afternoon, August 7, 2002–2:30 p.m.

- I inform dad via an Instant Messenger conversation that I talked with Karla and I am extremely worried about her. Her mania has worsened and has consumed her thoughts. I ask him if he has talked with her. She has shared similar stories with him about the spiritual journey she's been on. He's also concerned. He has a trip scheduled to meet my mom in New Jersey tomorrow morning, where they are scheduled to visit their good friends, Ginny and Tom, and make a trip to Ground Zero. He suggests that he might change the trip and go to Oklahoma instead. We both agree the importance of her continuing on her medication and seeing a doctor.

- Dad speaks with Karla and can feel the same manic attitude. However, Karla seems much calmer now and realizes that she needs to get to the doctor tomorrow. She is very convincing that she has everything under control. Dad does not change his scheduled trip to New Jersey.

Wednesday Night, August 7–11:30 p.m.–11:35 p.m.

- Karla calls me randomly. I am in the middle of celebrating my birthday with friends in St. Louis. I go outside and we talk briefly. She does not want to talk long, only to tell me that she was reminiscing about past birthdays. She says that she just had a party that was wonderful. Several of her friends are still there and she is making a fun-fetti cake. I am somewhat concerned by the randomness of her call and can certainly sense the mania. The degree is not nearly as much as it was earlier in the morning. I am convinced she will see her doctor tomorrow.

Thursday Afternoon, August 8–12:15 p.m.–12:45 p.m.

- I am at my house in St. Louis. I am currently in-between projects with Accenture, although a call earlier in the morning suggests a next possible assignment. I am working on a task for the St. Louis Accenture office. My cell phone rings and the caller ID indicates the call is coming from Karla's house. I answer. Art is the caller. He informs me of frightening news. Karla has left Stillwater and we are unsure of her whereabouts.

- Art explains the occurrences of the night and the story is slowly pieced together. He says that Karla was in her most manic state in the early hours of the morning, and he and Marie (Karla's other roommate) did not know what to do. They had been dealing with her in this state for over forty-eight hours, a mentally exhausting task. Karla wakes up Art at 5:30 a.m. looking for her car keys. She tells him that she is going to her friend Billy's and that she left a note explaining everything to Art. There was no stopping her and she left for Billy's, a friend in Stillwater.

- Art read the incoherent letter and realized that they were in trouble. He immediately called Billy and asked him to have Karla call when she arrived. Karla called back shortly thereafter and said that she just wanted to sleep. She promised Art she would go to the doctor later in the day to get her medicine.

- At 9:30 a.m., Karla called Art again. She told him that she was breaking her promise and was going to Tulsa to see Lonnie. She had not slept at all. Art tried to reason with her and tell her not to go, but she would not listen. She was gone.

- Art and Marie do not have a car, and Karla is now in her most manic state yet. She has slept very little in the past seventy-two hours, has $0 to her name, no credit cards, has less than a half a tank of gas in an unreliable car that she is now supposedly driving ninety miles to Tulsa. Our fears are many during this volatile situation. Will Karla actually go to Tulsa? What's to say she will not drive to another city? During her past manic episode she got off a bus in Tucumcari, New Mexico, ended up in jail and ultimately in a mental hospital. Will she have enough gas to make it to any destination? Will her mechanically challenged car be able to make the ninety miles? What will happen if she is stranded on the side of the road? Who will pick her up? We have absolutely no way to contact her. Does Lonnie understand her current state of mind? What people will take advantage of an attractive young woman in an unstable state of mind?

- The seriousness of this situation is starting to become clear to me. Art, who has handled things very well so far, has panic in his voice. He called me for help. Internally, I tell myself that this call is just the beginning. I'm fully engaged now and am ready to see this thing through. We discuss our options. First and foremost is our attempt to find Karla. Our biggest fear is whom she might be with at this time. Unfortunately, she has an extremely abusive past with some people in Tulsa. She once had connections to a group that included several people and ex-boyfriends who physically and mentally abused her. In her previous manic state four years ago, these individuals contributed greatly to her mania. Karla has always had a power over men. She has charmed them and they have abused her. She always wanted to help them since she so beautifully sees the good in people, and rarely the bad. If she encounters any of those people in her current state of mind, the outcome could be tragic.

- The scariest part is that we are helpless. Art does not have a means of transportation to get to Tulsa, and I am currently in St. Louis. We do not even know if she is in Tulsa. My mom has been in New Jersey for the past few days, and my dad is en route there now. Art also reveals that he and Marie tried to call Karla's psychiatrist at the OSU student health center earlier this morning. They discovered that Karla lied about the scheduled appointment to see her doctor today but the doctor is on vacation until Aug. 13. They speak briefly with Jack Davis at the health center. Getting the necessary medicine to Karla now becomes an even deeper concern. It is the only thing that might bring her back to reality.

- Art and I discuss our options and we determine the following course of action: 1) I will call and leave a message for Lonnie, whom I met on a visit to Tulsa two years ago. Still unclear as to the so-called spiritual revival Karla has experienced with him, we think it's very possible Karla will first go see him. 2) I will call the student health center at OSU and talk with Jack Davis. Perhaps by having a family member call and explain the situation, our medical options will become clearer. 3) I will call my mom in NJ and notify her of the situation. Art and Marie are not Karla's family, this is our problem and we need to start making the decisions.

- Art will call Mandy Hayes, another good friend of Karla who lives in Oklahoma City. We feel it's possible Karla would try to contact her or may travel to visit her. We want to prepare Mandy for any possibility and make sure she notifies us if Karla contacts her. Our goal is to touch base with all the people whom Karla may contact during her mania and make sure they know that she is certainly in a fragile state of mind.

- Art and I agree to update each other with any developments.

Thursday Afternoon, August 8–12:45 p.m.–1:10 p.m.

- 12:45 p.m.—I call Lonnie in Tulsa and there is no answer. I leave an urgent message describing Karla's condition and explaining that I need to talk with him as soon as possible. I tell him that Karla talked to Art in Stillwater around 9:30 a.m. saying that she was going to Tulsa to visit Lonnie. Normal travel time from Stillwater to Tulsa is about ninety minutes. Why is Karla not at Lonnie's by now? Were they possibly at lunch? What if Karla hears my voice on the answering machine? Will she become belligerent and even more distant? I hang up and it's all starting to sink in now. I'm beginning to lose some faith. I do not know how this will turn out.

- 12:50 p.m.—I call the OSU Student Health office and there is no answer, only a recorded message saying the office will re-open at 1:00.

- 12:55–1:05 p.m.—I reach mom in NJ. I catch her on a beach with her best friend Ginny. Mom had been aware of Karla's recent episode, but was not at all aware of the recent developments and the increased severity of the problem during the past twenty-four hours. She's very concerned as she was deeply involved with Karla during her first manic breakdown four years ago. She confirms that dad is on a plane and is scheduled to land in Newark within the hour. She will drive back to Ginny's house in Princeton and will arrive there in about two hours. She will tell dad the situation and they will call me. I suggest for the first time, that I think someone from the family needs to get to Oklahoma as soon as possible, probably dad.

- 1:10 p.m.—I am alone in my house and my mind is racing. I have tried repeatedly to leave a message on my dad's cell phone, but his service is the worst in the history of cell phones. Unable to leave a message, I went into my kitchen, and for the first time in this ordeal, I nearly lost it. I prayed out loud and asked God to help us.

Thursday Afternoon, August 8–1:15 p.m.–1:35 p.m.

- My cell phone rings and the caller ID is from my sister's house. It's not Karla or Art, it is Marie. I met Marie one time on a visit to Tulsa two years ago. Karla has spoken of her often. She's had an up-and-down relationship with Karla, but has certainly been one of her closest friends lately. She recently ended a marriage and has been living with Karla in Stillwater.

Karla's willingness to help anyone in need certainly shines through again. Marie expresses her deep concern over Karla and the situation right now. She's the first person I have talked to other than Art who has seen Karla during the past forty-eight manic hours. She, too, is shocked and amazed at Karla's behavior and feels completely helpless. She and Art have tried everything during the past two days and Karla will not listen. She is in her own world. They've gotten very little sleep. I begin to get a better grasp of the way Karla has acted recently. All of the symptoms I discussed with Art yesterday have occurred. It becomes clear as we talk that it will be extremely difficult for anyone to get through to Karla right now. We agree wholeheartedly that the only individual that Karla would not completely rebel against right now is my dad. I promise Marie that he will be involved shortly.

- Art then comes on the phone and tells the most important news of the day. Karla just called him from The Gypsy Café, a coffee shop in Tulsa. She said nothing more except that she was there. We have an initial sigh of relief because we now know where she is. Then, more questions and fears set in. Who is she with? We have no idea. How long will she be there? She could bolt out the door at any minute. What can we do?

- Art and I talk in our most emotional conversation yet. He begins to break down and talk about possible hospitals for Karla. He is keenly aware of the mental brutalization and rape (not physical) that Karla experienced when she was institutionalized four years ago at public state hospitals. Art expresses his sadness that things are not going to work out for them in terms of their relationship, but knows that he just can't let her continue to put him through this. I agree completely, and though it's disheartening to know that Karla is losing a protector in Art, I know that he has to do what is best for him in this relationship. His love for her is still apparent, though. He asks me to promise that that they will treat her right if she goes to another hospital. Spend whatever money necessary so she can get the best treatment. I assure him that we will only do what is best for Karla. How could we possibly not, I think to myself.

• It becomes clear to me during these conversations with Art and Marie that though we are very different people, we all share the same strong desire for Karla's well-being. She touches people in so many different ways when she is the person we all know she is. It's also clear that without Art and Marie's support during the past forty-eight hours, Karla would not be alive right now. As I thank Art for what he's done, I finally lose it and break down. I rarely do this. I pulled myself together and we began discussing our next steps.

• As I talk with Art, I research the location of the Gypsy Café in Tulsa on the Internet. I find the location and phone number. We discuss possibly calling them, but rule that out. If we appear as if we are trying to track her down, she will likely leave. Now that we know where she is, our best alternative is to have someone who is aware of the situation and is looking out for Karla's best interests to join her. Even though Karla will likely not respond favorably to Art showing up in Tulsa, we decide that he will look into the possibility of renting a car to drive to Tulsa. We just need to get her to a doctor who can get her medication. This has become our focus. We are trying to think of people in Tulsa who could go to her right now.

• I'm still on the phone with Art and a thought pops into my head. Looking back, I truly think God was working here. I thought of the Swiney's. This is a large family in Tulsa all of whom were good friends with Karla throughout high school and beyond. Three of their children, two girls and one boy, all attended high school with us. Karla had a special bond with all of them, the other siblings, and the parents. She spoke of them often and always visited when she was in Tulsa. Apparently, Karla had attended Mass with Mr. Swiney when she was in town the previous week. He had sensed that something was not right with her.

- Over a year ago, I paid $10.00 for a phone look-up service for all residential listed numbers in the United States. Today, it finally paid off. I found the Swiney's number online. Art completely agreed they would be the best people to contact. I will call them and see if they could find Karla at the Gypsy Café.

Thursday Afternoon, August 8–1:35 p.m.–1:50 p.m.

- I call the Swiney residence. Though I know their children, I had only met the parents a few brief times. Looking back, it never even occurred to me that maybe they wouldn't be home. Or that the line would be busy. God was with us. Mrs. Swiney answered the phone immediately and as soon as I said who I was, she knew why I was calling. Karla was like another daughter to them.

- As I explained the events of the past forty-eight hours, I broke down again for the second time of the day. Mrs. Swiney couldn't have been more gracious, concerned, or willing to help. She said, "We knew Karla was ill right now, but we still love her." I explained to her that we thought Karla might still be at The Gypsy Café. She knew exactly where it was. All we needed right now was someone to keep an eye on Karla and make sure she was safe.

- We knew time was of the essence, so we discussed briefly how she or her husband would intervene with Karla. I explained that I honestly did not think Karla would question why the Swineys happened to show up at the Café. She would think of it merely as a coincidence or a spiritual sign. On this one, I actually agreed with Karla. The Swineys certainly would be spiritual angels if they found Karla. However, it was still a big risk that Karla would still be there, and, even if she was, who knows how she would react. Mrs. Swiney was on her way.

Thursday Afternoon, August 8–1:50 p.m.–2:00 p.m.

- I wanted to find out more about the manic phase Karla was experiencing right now. How long would it last? Is there any medication that can stop it immediately? What should we do if we find her? How do we intervene?

- I called a good friend of mine with whom I went to college, Susanne Rosenberg, a registered head nurse in St. Louis. She met Karla a couple of times through me. Medically speaking, she knows her stuff. More importantly, she just knows people. Rarely though does she answer her cell phone on a Thursday afternoon … not today, however. She answered right away. God was with us.

- Typical of Susanne, she was in the middle of doing good in our world. She was at the STL airport ready to board a plane for Chicago with several cancer-stricken children for a weekend trip. In the midst of controlling some screaming kids, she still had a few minutes to talk and reaffirmed my thoughts. She said that the mania could last a few more days or could end abruptly. There's no telling. The Effexor she needs will not take effect in her system for several weeks. It will be impossible to reason with Karla now. Our only real option is to get her to some kind of professional help, whether it be a hospital or a psychiatric treatment center. Susanne is rarely wrong.

Thursday Afternoon, August 8–2:00 p.m.–3:00 p.m.

- I now have a chance to call the OSU student health center. As Jack Davis is not available, I am put in contact with Dr. Susan Burks, who is the Director of University Counseling Services.

- Initially, she sites several legal reasons (all valid) why she can't confirm or deny anything about one of her patients. I feel like this conversation will go nowhere, but I begin to tell her the story and events of the past few days. She listens and becomes more open to talking. She has a heart. Not every doctor does. We begin to discuss our options for moving forward. She is certainly in agreement with getting her into a safe place and having a responsible family look after her. We hope Mrs. Swiney has found her, but we have no idea.

- Dr. Burks passes on good information: 1) We need to make sure Karla signs a waiver allowing her family members to have access to her files. This would also allow OSU to tell us her recent history with her psychiatrist. 2) Dr. Burks highly recommends that Karla be taken to St. Francis or St. John's emergency room as soon as possible. There, she will be advised by the doctor on duty who will likely contact a psychiatrist. That individual will determine if Karla is harmful to herself or society and whether or not Karla will be admitted to an institution. This is the only way Karla can get the medication she needs, especially with her psycharist on vacation. 3) She discusses the recent problems the state of Oklahoma has had with public mental institutions. The Government has cut funding tremendously. They are in bad shape. Way understaffed. Patients are escorted by police in handcuffs and shackles. This is the only way they are admitted. A public institution will not be a pleasant experience for Karla. It is what she experienced four years ago. 4) Insurance will be an issue for Karla since she doesn't have any. She is not covered under my parents anymore. Some private institutions require insurance for admittance. It is possible to check in, receiving a no-pay bed. All institutions are required by law to have at least a few of these for people in Karla's situation; however, if this is only in a public institution, we shouldn't do it.

- We discuss at length our next biggest dilemma. If Karla is found, how do we intervene? How do we convince her that she needs the meds and she needs the hospital. Everyone who has encountered her in the past seventy-two hours knows she needs both remedies. Dr. Burks explains the two ways to be admitted—voluntary and involuntary. Obviously, voluntary is better as Karla signs a paper admitting herself. Involuntary uses a court system and judge to admit her as long as she is considered a risk to society. Past cases and files would help with this. OSU would certainly be willing to supply them.

- It's becoming clear that perhaps the biggest challenge of this ordeal will be the intervention. Karla will not be easy to convince. She can be so stubborn sometimes. And right now, she thinks everything is fine and nothing is wrong with her. She believes everything is wrong with everyone else and the world.

- Dr. Burks will have Jack Davis call me later. She is on board with our case and ready to help. I can call her as necessary.

Thursday Afternoon, August 8–3:00 p.m.–3:15 p.m.

- As I end my conversation with Dr. Burks, my cell phone indicates a new message. It's from Mr. Swiney; his wife found Karla at the coffee shop and she is safe at their home. What an amazing relief! I immediately call him back at his office.

- I explain the full story to Mr. Swiney, he had only heard bits and pieces from his wife. You'd think that I'd be able to say it all without a problem by now, but again I get a bit choked up. I am just touched by their deep concern and love for Karla. I explain to him my conversation with the doctors and inform him that it looks like we will try to admit her into a Tulsa hospital either tonight or tomorrow. I still need to get in touch with my parents to confirm this.

- I ask him in the interim to try to make sure that Karla stays at the Swiney house. My dad will hopefully be there late tonight or tomorrow morning. I decide that we still do not want Karla to know that our family is involved with anything. We do not want to set her off. We simply want to listen and make sure she is safe. This is much easier said than done as I fear Karla can take off at any time. He is in complete agreement.

Thursday Afternoon, August 8–3:15 p.m.–3:25 p.m.

- I call Art and Marie to update them. They are very relieved Karla is safe with the Swiney's for now. I tell Art it certainly is not necessary for him to go to Tulsa anymore, unless he wants to. He will stay in Stillwater. We are all in agreement that getting Karla admitted into a private hospital where she can get on her medication is the proper course of action.

- Lonnie has not called me back from my original message, but he has been in contact with Art and Marie. They informed him of Karla's extreme state right now. He understands and realizes she needs professional help. He will contact us if she contacts him. This is very good news.

- Marie and I discuss Karla's job and her incident with Ron. We are both unclear as to what really happened that day. I ask Marie to follow-up with Karla's supervisor, Rob Barnes, to find out if Karla is still employed and if it's possible she could have medical insurance coverage.

Thursday Afternoon, August 8–3:25 p.m.–4:00 p.m.

- I finally get a hold of dad on his cell phone. He is at Tom Cusack's office in New Jersey. Tom is Ginny's husband. Dad is unaware of today's events as he has not yet talked to mom. I call him back at Tom's office and tell him that we will have to make some decisions very fast.

- I give him a condensed version of the previous ten pages in this chronology. I look up possible flights for him on the Internet for tonight, but realize it will be difficult to make the connection. Dad will go meet Mom, Ginny, and Tom, discuss the scenarios, and fly to Tulsa in the morning.

- It's very comforting to have my parents fully involved now. They have handled this before. Perhaps I got the ball rolling on this today, but that was only because I knew the circumstances at the time. I know that they are the ones who are going to have to carry this over the finish line. And I know they will.

Thursday Afternoon, August 8–4:15 p.m.–5:15 p.m.

- I receive a call from Jack Davis at OSU Health Center. His title is the Coordinator of Counseling Services. He has been involved with counseling for fifteen years and will receive his PhD in a few months. He makes me aware of the legal issues which I know he is faced with during our conversation, but you can tell right away Jack has a big heart and will help us in any way he can.

- I again explain Karla's history and recent events. He has never met her. We discuss many of the symptoms of bipolar, and he sheds some more light on the sickness. It is good to be reaffirmed regarding all the thoughts we had and the actions we took throughout the day.

- He echoes many of the same sentiments of Dr. Burks and adds this insight: 1) Perhaps using the police might be the only way to admit Karla, if she is completely opposed to checking into a hospital. The police can pick her up on a well-check and take her to the ER. 2) We should be able to get a mandated seventy-two-hour admittance as long as a doctor is convinced Karla is a threat to herself and/or society.

- I ask him if he could maybe talk to whatever hospital we take her to tomorrow, and he says that is not really protocol, but will help in any way he can. He will attempt to contact her psychiatrist to find out more about Karla. He also gave me an OSU public safety number that will page him if we need to contact him tonight.

Thursday Afternoon, August 8–5:30 p.m.–6:00 p.m.

- I have my final conversation of the day with Marie and Art and talk to Marie. She has contacted Rob Barnes, and it looks as if Karla's insurance will not cover her since she maintained only fifteen working hours for the past month. For all practical purposes, she is no longer employed there.

- I want to get to the bottom of some of the manic thoughts and stories Karla has discussed in recent days. Marie tells of a recent incident in which Karla threw away Art and Marie's toothbrushes and toothpaste. When questioned about it, Karla replied, "What really is toothpaste?" Marie and I discuss the spiritual connection that Karla has been speaking about.

We try to get to the bottom of this, but it's clear Karla has not been consistent in her stories. Marie explains that Justin called several times right after the cruise, but Karla would not talk to him. She doesn't think they have talked at all. A package from Justin arrived in the mail today. It's my opinion that we make sure Karla does not open or see that package, as it will likely conjure false images from a person she has known for a week and considers to be a possible spiritual soul mate.

- Marie and Art are exhausted. I tell them to sleep and try to relax. They have done enough. It is in the hands of the Swineys and our family, and of course Karla's mind. I will update them with any developments tomorrow.

Thursday Evening, August 8–6:00 p.m.–6:30 p.m.

- I call Mandy Hayes to update her and get an understanding of this spiritual revival. I have talked to her maybe once since high school. We certainly did not have the same group of friends in high school. She currently lives with her friend Sunshine.

- Mandy is very rational and very glad I called. Likewise, talking with her helped tremendously. She is concerned about Karla after seeing her last night. As far as the spiritual connection last week that Karla said Mandy was a part of—this was news to Mandy. It's scary to think this is true, but proves that Karla's spiritual connection with six other people was clearly only in her own mind. The bipolar manic mind knows no limits.

- Mandy is completely willing to help in any way she can and is aware that Karla will likely approach her when she is in a more stable condition. She also understands the importance of always advising Karla to stay on her meds. I will keep her updated throughout the next couple days via e-mail.

Thursday Evening, August 8–6:30 p.m.

- My roommate, John, gets home from work and overhears a bit of what's going on. He knows some of Karla's past and has met her in the past year. He's been aware of what's been happening the past couple days before today. I fill him in on today's events. He's great. Best roommate I've ever had and a close friend. Glad he was in town today; it helped me. Suggested maybe I/we should go to Tulsa. Might be a possibility depending on what happens the next couple of days.

Thursday Evening, August 8–7:00 p.m.-7:45 p.m.

- I call mom and dad in New Jersey and talk with both of them at the same time. I give them the final updates from the day and start talking about next steps and the best way to intervene. I suggest maybe it's better if the Swiney's do it, just because Karla sometimes struggles to listen to her family members—especially when she knows they might be right. Perhaps she will take the request better from people outside the family. I provide the numbers of several hospitals in the Tulsa area. I decide to start working on the chronology of events, which I start around 8:00 and I'm doing now at 9:28.

- They will do the following: 1) decide who will go to Tulsa tomorrow and who will intervene, 2) contact the Swine's , 3) call the hospitals to prepare them for Karla's visit, and 4) contact Rob Barnes about Karla's current employment status.

Thursday Evening, August 8–9:30 p.m.

- Dad calls back with some updates. 1) He and mom will both fly to Tulsa in the morning and arrive around 10:30 a.m.. Dad will be the only one who will try to intervene and convince Karla to voluntarily commit herself. 2) Hillcrest hospital looks like the best place. The night doctor was informed of the situation. It seems there might be an open bed. Her past experience should be enough to warrant admittance, but nothing is

for sure. 3) Karla does not have medical insurance through her
employer.

- Unfortunately, there is no answer at the Swiney's right now.
  Dad will keep trying. We hope they are just out to dinner with
  Karla, but also know it's very possible Karla could have left.
  The Swiney's have taken her car keys (at my request) so, hope-
  fully, if Karla does try to leave, she won't be able to go far.

Thursday Evening, August 8–9:45 p.m.

- Dad calls back and was able to get in touch with the Swiney's.
  They were at dinner with Karla. Sadly, it now seems as if her
  condition is even worse. Karla is now having conversations
  with people who are not there. Mrs. Swiney has said Karla
  tried to go to sleep but was unable to. Fortunately, Mrs.
  Swiney is nocturnal, so she will likely be able to stay awake
  with her most of the night. Still, the biggest fear is that Karla
  will try to leave sometime before my parents get there in the
  morning. Apparently, she still has not comprehended why she
  is at the Swiney house. Hopefully, she will not.

Thursday Evening, August 8–10:00 p.m.

- Cardinals finally win, 5–3. Break 7 game losing streak. Thank
  God.

Friday Morning, August 9–2:45 a.m.

- I am finished writing this chronology for now, and I'm ready
  to send it to Mom and Dad so they can read it on the plane in
  the morning. Ginny actually calls to make sure it's on the way.
  It's hard to describe why I felt so compelled to write this
  tonight. I've never been much of a writer, but perhaps in some
  small way it might help the healing process for Karla in the
  future. At least that is my hope now. People remember certain
  dates in life—12/25, 9/11. I will always remember 8/8—this
  day has changed my life forever.

Friday Morning, August 9–8:30 a.m.

- Dad calls from the airport at a stopover on the way to Tulsa. There is finally good news and possible closure to the day's events. Mr. Swiney has left a message for dad saying that Karla is now safe and in a Tulsa hospital, under physician's care. At this time, we have no details as to how she got there. The Swiney's will pick up my parents at the airport in Tulsa at 10:30 a.m. and dad will call me.

Friday Morning, August 9–8:40 a.m.

- I receive a call from Mrs. Swiney. She called to tell me Karla is safe and at the hospital and to recap some of the night's events. What a relief! I'm grateful that we decided that the Swiney's could do the intervention if they felt they could. All that mattered was that she was admitted.

- Mrs. Swiney explains the events that led to Karla's admission. As the night progressed, Karla became even more delusional. She continued conversations with people that weren't there and finally reached a point of extreme fear. She was unable to sleep and had been awake for over seventy-two straight hours. She wrestled out loud with what to do and became very frightened. She felt like she was being trapped and said she needed to get out of the house. The times are not clear yet, but I think around 2:00 or 3 a.m. she wanted to go to the coffee shop. The Swiney's got her in the car and rather than driving to a coffee shop, drove to Hillcrest Hospital. Fortunately, Karla did not seem to understand the diversion or where she was going.

- Karla walked into the hospital and the nurses who saw her in the waiting room could tell she was extremely manic. Karla was talking wildly. The doctor on duty saw the same thing. After talking with the doctor, Karla said at one point, "okay, it's time for me to leave now." The doctor replied, "No, I don't think so." She was admitted to Hillcrest Hospital even though their inpatient program was full, and she has since been transferred to another hospital in Tulsa that had some availability. She has taken medication that will sedate her and allow her finally to sleep.

• My parents and the Swiney's will update me later, but for now everything we had hoped for has fallen into place. I'm unsure as to how long Karla will stay at this hospital or what treatment she will need, but my parents will likely figure that out when they arrive. Though I finally feel more at ease with this situation, I certainly have the anxiety that this is nowhere near over. This is day one of another long, painful recovery time. During her last episode, it was not until a month after she left the hospital that she attempted suicide and was miraculously saved by about one hour.

• Right now, I'm just struck by the sadness of this relapse. Karla was doing so well. She was a semester away from graduating, had established a steady job, had found some quality friends, and was making high grades. She had truly turned the corner and was a joy to be around. Our family was the closest it had been in years following the cruise. I just hope she can get back to that point as soon as possible, but I know it will be a long, long journey. She just needs a break right now and needs to be strong in her thinking. She will likely feel very depressed over the next few weeks and the thought of that is very scary to me. She will likely question her reason for living. She needs to understand her purpose in life, and perhaps all the people that have been worried about her in the past forty-eight hours will show her that purpose.

Friday Morning, August 9–10:20 a.m.

• Lonnie from Tulsa calls me back. He has just received my message from yesterday. He also expresses his deep concern for Karla and knew that she was in bad shape. He saw her briefly at the Gypsy Café yesterday and agreed that Mrs. Swiney should take her. Lonnie had never experienced anyone in a manic state before and we discussed many of the warning signs. Since Karla stayed with him last week, he is now more aware of these signs. He witnessed many of them.

- Lonnie also confirms that he was not at all a part of this spiritual community Karla spoke so much about during her mania. This is not a surprise, as Mandy said the same thing. He is truly ready and willing to help her in any way that he can in the future and knows that any time Karla would discuss not taking her medication would be an extremely dangerous warning sign. Lonnie has helped Karla tremendously in the past and will be there again in the future. He is a very good, caring man. I will send him this chronology so that he understands a bit more about the warning signs for Karla and everything that has happened the past two days.

Friday Afternoon, August 9–12:00

- Parents arrive in Tulsa. They find Karla at Tulsa Crisis Center. The doctor there will not admit her. She received Haldol and other drugs to sedate her. My parents try desperately to get her admitted into a good treatment center in Tulsa, but nothing is available. We feel this is the only thing that will help her in the short term since she will be supervised around the clock. It is not easy to watch Karla during this time. We are not equipped to keep an eye on her twenty-four hours a day. She insists that it is not necessary, but we know that it is—only because we love her and want to make sure she is safe. Karla can be extremely convincing and stubborn, even when she is manic, and she refuses to attend treatment. Our hands are tied. We can not force her, and the treatment center will not take her. It is such a helpless feeling again because our lives have become focused only on helping her, but she will not agree to stay and, for a variety of reasons, the doctor won't admit her.

- Karla sleeps finally from 12:30 p.m.–8:30 p.m. at the Swiney's. My parents and the Swiney's discuss what is next. It is difficult because much of that is trying to figure out what Karla will want and say. Do we take her to St. Louis? Better treatment facilities? What if Karla has an episode on the plane and disrupts the flight attendants and other passengers? She could be arrested with the latest post 9/11 security rules. What if she goes to St. Louis and hates it here? Will she run away?

- I talk to dad three times with updates, and I keep Art and Marie in the loop and prepare them for a possible trip to Stillwater. Karla has nothing with her in Tulsa—no clothes, etc. She hardly even comprehends this at this time. Nothing matters to her.

Saturday Morning, August 10–9:00 a.m.

- I receive a message from mom. Karla, mom, and dad have flown from Tulsa to St. Louis on an early morning flight. We could no longer disrupt the lives of the Swiney's, and without a hospital willing to take Karla in Oklahoma, this was really the only option. We know that she will need twenty-four-hour watch during the next couple weeks until her medicine truly kicks in. This is a daunting and exhausting task for our family, one that she doesn't even remotely grasp, but one that we certainly will take on without any hesitation. Our lives continue to be put on hold.

- I have a long conversation with Art and fill him in on the latest. He's thankful for what we've done and he says he will contact Karla soon. I also leave a message for Lonnie.

Saturday Afternoon, August 10

- Karla leaves me a voice mail mid-afternoon inviting me over to my parents' house and saying they might go to a play tonight. Her message is brief, but you can certainly sense the mania. She has no idea what we have been through the past three days.

- I talk with mom and dad on the phone. They say that Karla has had a better day, but she is still manic. I plan to come over in the evening for dinner, and we agree that renting a comedy movie would be a good activity for tonight.

Saturday Evening, August 10

- I arrive at my parents and see Karla for the first time. She's been napping on the couch. She sees me and wakes up. She stands to hug me and begins to cry softly on my shoulder. I hold in my emotion. It's so amazing to actually see her after all I have thought about her in the past seventy-two hours. I ask her if she is scared, and she says she's not anymore. I wish I could say the same. It takes just a few seconds of being around her to know she is not well right now. And deep down she knows it, too. Call it a twin thing, but I can sense she feels it.

- We have dinner and I do a lot of observing of Karla. She seems pleasant, sometimes even laughing and happy. But certainly still in the mania. I'm struck most by her hyperactivity and inability to finish a story or stay in one place. I count the number of times she gets up from the table during our thirty-minute dinner. Seven. Usually, just to help everyone. Get another plate, get her cigarettes, clear a dish. Then she walks out on the patio to "be with the locusts." She sits for several minutes and waves at me occasionally through the window. I watch her out of the corner of my eye the whole time. I still have this fear she will run away. How can I not? Movement is extremely vital to her right now.

- Mom and dad fill me in on the day as Karla sits outside. When Karla wasn't sleeping, my parents tried to keep her busy—either with chores around the house or projects. Karla washes mom's car and earns $5—the only money she has to her name right now. My parents explain that they will be taking her to a doctor on Monday in Belleville to get her more medication, namely Effexor. She only has one pill right now to take and she refuses to take it because she says it makes her jittery. This is extremely worrisome to me as medication is the only thing that will bring her back to normal. My parents are prepared to take her to the emergency room on Sunday, if she gets out of control. Sunday is a day that scares me a lot.

- Karla continues to be unable to focus on one activity or conversation. She has now changed clothes three times since I've been there. She says this is normal everyday life, but of course to me it's a bit strange. We watch a movie and Karla falls asleep for most of it. My mom, weary from the day, goes to bed halfway through the movie. Karla is awakened when the phone rings. I knew exactly who it was and it scared me. The caller was Justin, returning a previous call from Karla. My dad answers and quickly gives the phone to Karla. Justin was the only person of Karla's close friends whom I had been unable to contact to warn about her manic episodes. He is deeply in love with Karla after meeting her on the cruise. They knew each other for one week. She has made reference to him being her soul mate and vice versa. It's scary to me that they are talking and Justin has no idea what is going on. He believes they have deep spiritual connections and I'm afraid he might come to visit and take Karla with him. Or Karla could just decide to go there at any minute (he lives in Madison, WI).

- Karla goes into her room and I express my deep concerns with my dad. He understands. I had no way of getting Justin's number until now. I've wanted to call him. We come up with the following plan. Dad will go into Karla's room and casually take the notebook with Justin's number. I will program it into my phone. As soon as Karla gets off the phone with him, I will take Karla outside and talk to her about her plans with Justin. My fear is that he will come here soon or she will leave. Then I will call Justin and tell him about Karla's current state. I dread this conversation as I know that Justin wants to be with Karla, and I fear he will not understand my reason for calling. Dad goes in the room and gets the notebook; I program the number into my cell phone. The one good thing about Karla's current state is that she is so focused on one thing, she sometimes misses the obvious, or she will forget to ask. She didn't even think to ask dad, "why are you taking my notebook?'" Sad to say, but the only way we can help her now is to use some of her mania to help us.

- Karla ends a brief conversation with Justin and comes screaming out of the room in joy. She is singing and chanting in exuberance, but she only says "my soul mate will be here soon. He's got to finish up his work, put on his work boots, but then he'll be here." I am not surprised she reacts like this. I've seen Karla when she likes a guy or if she feels a connection with him. It's 100%, all or nothing. She goes all out. There is no reasoning or stopping her. The feeling is all that matters. I think to myself, "Gee, Karla, how about a few dates to get to know someone, then maybe become a bit more serious? Hello!" This, however, is not the relationship pattern of Karla Smith.

- I ask Karla to come outside with me as I leave. She insists on me driving around the block as we talk. Movement again is necessary. Pure mania. I calmly ask Karla questions about Justin. I feel bad in a way because I'm only trying to prepare myself for the phone call I will make to him as soon as I leave, but I know this has to be done. Karla and I have a deep, almost frightening conversation for several laps around the block. (Yes, she says I need to keep making the same damn circle. Over. And over. And over.) I ask her about Justin. A few of her replies: "He is a mirror of me. We are soul mates. He is me." Jokingly, I say, wow that's scary. Two Karla's on one planet. She laughs. She knows I have to continue to tease her; it's always been my role in the family. And I know I want to keep the mood light, otherwise she will tell me nothing. I ask if that means Justin is also bipolar. She says, "Of course not, at least I don't think so." My worst fears are realized as she explains Justin is coming to get her soon, "it's just not quite time yet." I know that I need to talk to him as soon as possible. Our conversation goes in several directions as we discuss school, mom and dad, and the immediate future. Karla asks me to find out how much apartments cost in St. Louis. One bedroom, one bath. I tell her probably $500 or $600. She says, no problem, that's nothing. I think, "Hello, you have no money or job." Karla just is not adding everything up right now. She says, I'm going to get a job on Monday at "some little place". Well maybe Tuesday if all the doctor stuff takes a long time Monday. Sadly, I know that Karla won't be working anywhere where she could afford a $500 month apartment for quite awhile. I suspect that within the next week or so, she will ask to borrow money from me. I fear this question because there is no right answer. Do I bail her out financially? I can't just leave her on the street. Karla brings up Mandy and the relation to the Siamese twins separated at birth. She tells me that she believes Mandy was her twin and they were separated at birth. I am not her twin. I've already talked to Mandy about this and clearly she disagrees. They, of course, are not twins, not even metaphorically, even though they are good friends. Karla talks more and more about her desire not to be in Tulsa. She makes a reference to "Haldol in the hand" and points to a small scab where she received the shot two days ago. She says one day she will tell me everything. Everything about why she can't be in Oklahoma, about the South American mafia that is after her. About how taking Haldol in the hand is her punishment. Her mania is racing. She says "Karla … me somewhere else." Karla does not feel safe in Oklahoma. After awhile, she needs to get out of the car. Our conversation is ending. I try to talk to her more, more just for me. I want to tell her about my life. I want to tell her about Angela, a girl I have been dating from Madrid, Spain, coming to St. Louis. But she can't listen. It's only her right now. She asks nothing about my life. This is what I hate most about this mania and when she is not on her medication. The sister I love, who always listens and knows what to say, and knows me is not there. It is only her world and we have to live in it. It's a selfish thought I know, but also human. I maintained our conversation so that she knows I'm looking out for her. As she left, I asked her to please take her medication. To do it for me. I know the meds are the only thing that will bring her back. I told her to listen to mom and dad, and if she felt things weren't working out with them to call me. I wanted her to call me before she does anything irrational. I know they won't give her problems, but she needs me to be the outlet if necessary. As we leave, I tell her I love her and she's happy because I usually joke about saying it. This time though I say it out of fear. I'm more scared after seeing her than I was before I saw her. Karla does thank me for everything, she knows that I had a big part in helping her the past few days, she's just not sure of the details. I tell her that someday I will tell her everything. Clearly, I'm thinking of this journal I'm writing. Tomorrow is crucial, and so are the next two weeks. I'm not looking forward to them.

- I call Justin and his mom answers. Justin isn't there. I explain everything to his mom. She has a cousin who is bipolar. She's on our side. She gives me the number where Justin is. She says that she will help in any way she can if Karla travels to Madison.

- I call Justin. I know this will be an important conversation. Inside I'm scared. All of Karla's other friends that I spoke with on the phone actually saw Karla in the past week during her mania. They totally understood my fears and concerns and were all very willing to help. Justin hasn't seen anything, only experienced the connection with a completely different Karla for one week on a cruise ship. It will be hard to explain that she's not that same person now. Justin is twenty-five, very fast-talking (often you can't understand him), seems to be very intelligent and socially skilled, and believes very strongly in spiritual energy. Clearly, he's the type of person to which Karla would gravitate for a relationship. Justin is surprised to hear of Karla's condition, but doesn't say much. He does admit he was coming to see her this weekend in Oklahoma. I tell him that is not what she needs right now. Perhaps in a few weeks when she is normal, but now it could be catastrophic. He understands, but I don't fully trust him. He claims he felt a lot of energy from Karla this past Wednesday, but did not participate in any of the planned meditation activities that

Karla says took place over the past week. None of the other five people she has mentioned have participated. Justin says he will do what he can to help and not talk to Karla for a little while. He says he has never experienced anyone who is manic. He also admits Karla seemed extremely exuberant and jumpy on the phone tonight. He has not talked to her in over a week. I explain this is because she is still manic. I almost get the feeling from him that he wants to be manic with Karla and is somewhat jealous. I didn't want to bring this out, but I had to tell Justin of Karla's suicide attempt four years ago after being manic. He is starting to understand the severity of this. It's finally sinking in, or so he says. I tell him to please, please, please do not tell Karla that we talked; otherwise she could get extremely upset. That could be disastrous. I am only trying to do what is best for Karla here, and I think he believes that. I give him my cell phone number and ask him to call me whenever and I will update him on Karla's condition. It should not surprise Karla if he doesn't call her, as she said she doesn't know when he'll call again. Only that she'll be ready.

Sunday, August 11

- Karla spends an active day with mom and dad, which includes an evening visit from Sharon (her aunt) and Janie. I am unable to make it out to Belleville due to prior commitments. Karla is aware of this. However, she calls me three different times in a matter of eight hours (4:00 p.m.-midnight). On the phone she is still manic. She has started using e-mail again, searching for more outlets for her frantic energy. Last night, she sent an e-mail to several family and friends saying that she was now back from a "brief lovely hiatus" and wanted them to write. I don't think that's how I'd exactly describe the past week. Karla had earlier forwarded me a random spam e-mail about winning some car in Arkansas at a fair this weekend. She wants me to go there with her. She says that Justin is a "master of the Internet" and he was actually behind the spam message showing up in her inbox. Another manic delusion. I find this one rather comical as I work with computers all day and receive numerous similar e-mails. I explain to her that it's just a marketing initiative and she reluctantly agrees. Later in the evening Karla calls me and is very upset. She says she needs to get out. I explain to her that perhaps mom and dad are a bit stressed right now. They are only trying to help her. If they've only had one negative encounter over the weekend, that's pretty good. Karla agrees to focus on the positive. She understands and feels better about it. She calls me again around midnight saying she is scared about going to bed. She says it will be a long night. I tell her to try to relax and that tomorrow when she gets her medication, she will start feeling more at ease.

- I have conversations with two medical professionals with whom I am friends. They are not at all surprised by Karla's behavior. The fact that she even got off her medication in the first place is not a shock to them. Most bipolar individuals do it, and they say that it likely will happen again. They are extremely surprised however that Effexor was the only drug Karla had been taking to control it. They both said that most bipolar people need much stronger drugs, namely lithium. They say that we are treating her in the right way and we are doing everything we should be doing, but they believe that some kind of professional treatment is important.

Monday, August 12

- My parents and Karla make phone calls to mental health facilities in the Belleville area and discover that there is a waiting list and she can't see a doctor for medication at this time because she is not currently in a state of emergency. She is put on the waiting list with the possibility of receiving some attention in two to four weeks. The care for mental health patients across our country is so inadequate, it is scary.

- Dad phones Jack Davis at OSU and explains the situation and Karla's need for medication. He understands. Since Karla was a patient through OSU, he is able to prescribe a two-week supply of Effexor. The prescription is called into a pharmacy in Belleville. Karla gladly takes her first Effexor in the early afternoon. She will take this daily. Unfortunately, she is adamantly against taking any other drugs. In this regard, there is little we can do. She's the one who has to take it. Our hope is that she will continue to take the Effexor daily and the combination of the drug and Karla's mental belief that it is what she needs to make her better will do the trick. Karla also agrees to call her psychiatrist at OSU tomorrow. She will set up weekly appointments with her. As of now, it seems as if the long-term plan will be for her to return to Stillwater for this semester's classes. Of course, that is the plan for today ... it could change by the hour.

- I go to my parents' house on Monday evening to see Karla. I had talked with her briefly on the phone earlier and told her about a bipolar video I had just watched on MTV. She was excited about seeing it. When I got there, Karla was still deeply in the mania and was very upset. She had gotten in an argument with Art on the phone earlier in the night and she claimed she was beginning to feel trapped at my parents' house. She said she wanted to go back to Oklahoma. The four of us discussed this possibility, and it was clear by Karla's actions that she was starting to lose it. She had only been in Belleville now for two days and she said that it felt like weeks. She began screaming at us loudly, that she couldn't take being trapped, that she had to get home as soon as possible. She then pounded the couch and sobbed angrily. The three of us knew by her actions that we couldn't even consider letting Karla leave. Karla bolted from the living room saying in tears that she was fine and that she hated us and didn't want to talk to us. She went into her bedroom and slammed the door.

- My parents and I discussed the situation. It was so heartbreaking to see her mood swings change so dramatically, this time for the worst. When Karla gets like this, it is just so difficult to reason with her, but we knew that of course we had to keep an eye on her for fear of what might happen next. Since she was now at odds with my parents, I decided that I would go into Karla's room and try to calm her down. If all went well, I would ask her to come to my house in St. Louis as I thought she might perceive this as a bit more freedom for her, since that is what it seemed she desired.

• I went into Karla's room and she was sobbing on the phone with Lonnie. She repeatedly kept asking him to drive to Belleville now and rescue her, that her family was holding her hostage. I convinced her to hang up the phone because I wanted to talk to her and angrily she did. I said a little prayer silently before I started talking to her, because I knew this conversation would be an important one. Calmly I asked her why she had gotten so angry. She was defiant at first but after a couple minutes, she calmed down a little. For the first time in dealing with this situation, my emotions came out as I talked to her. I told her that all I wanted to do was look out for her. When she saw that, we connected. I told her that I missed most her being my friend and advisor during this time. For a brief moment it hit her how much we had all been doing to help her. We started talking about how she was feeling right now. She began opening up to me and though her delusional stories were difficult to listen to, I didn't dispute them. Finally, we moved into the living room and talked more. Our connection was strong and Karla knew that I was looking out for her. She also said that though she didn't realize it until now, I was part of her "soul family" and because of this "psychic energy" I had, she felt like she could let me in. Not sure if I'd describe it the same way, but I certainly will say that I always have and always will feel a special bond with my only sibling. During the course of our conversation, I tried to instill concrete thoughts in her manic mind. She said that she still felt the mania very strongly, but also admitted that she wanted it to stop—and would do anything to make it stop. I began creating a list of the things for her to accomplish in the next couple days, the first of which was to stop the mania. She agreed to stay the night at my house and also agreed to wait until Wednesday to go back to Stillwater. It was approaching 1:00 a.m. when we finally got to my house.

Tuesday, Aug. 13

- Karla slept for nearly nine hours, the most she has slept consecutively in over a week. I told her the night before that sleep would help fight the mania and for awhile it appeared to. Karla had one of her better days. Though she still had many manic thoughts and could not sit still, except to smoke a cigarette, she was calmer—although I was scared to let her out of my sight.

- I called Art and Marie to update them, mainly to inform them that Karla was doing better. Also wanted to tell them that she would be coming home tomorrow night. I was surprised by their negative reaction. Both Art and Marie expressed concern about her return to Stillwater and said they did not want to be responsible for what she might do. Clearly, the effects of Karla's manic episode in Stillwater last week had an extreme impact on them. They wanted her to be in a long-term treatment center. Though I agreed that would be the best, I explained to them that Karla simply would not do it and the availability was limited. The most difficult part of this process was that she had the legal right to make the decision about treatment and in her state of mind, she was nearly impossible to convince about anything. She is a twenty-six-year-old adult and when she's not in an extreme manic state, she is legally capable of making her own decisions. It's not like she's a child.

- It was mentally and physically exhausting watching her all day. Every five minutes she would ask me to do some minor task for her, whether it was turning on CNN, or country music, or listening to her theories, or looking something up on the internet. (She had become fearful of the Internet during this manic stage.) I had no problem doing these things as I was only trying to make her comfortable, but the stress of it all got to me, and I experienced a migraine headache. I was in rough shape for most of the morning and Karla was good about helping me. I'm glad she was there. Her true inner kindness still comes out even when she's outside reality.

• I created a color-printout document for her outlining the plan we had agreed to last night for the rest of the week. I thought it was important that she try to maintain a structure during her mania. It was difficult to get her to start following this list, but she did eventually start and she called her counseling office at OSU to set up an appointment for Thursday. Unfortunately, Jack Davis was not available and her psychiatrist was still on vacation, so Karla only spoke with the receptionist. I was a bit hesitant about this. Karla sounded very professional on the phone and said that she had booked an appointment with her psychiatrist for Thursday at 3:00. This was a sigh of relief as Karla agreed that if the psychiatrist prescribed more medication, Karla would listen and understand. The challenge would be getting her to that Thursday appointment. As we all had experienced the past seven days, she made several promises that she hasn't kept.

• Karla makes contact with her friend Billy in Stillwater late in the afternoon. Since she knew she was coming home tomorrow, and she knew she didn't want to live with Art and Marie, she told us that she would move in with Billy for awhile. Everything would be fine, no problem. Of course, I thought otherwise. No matter how good a friend you are, it's not likely you will allow someone who was just extremely manic to move into your one bedroom apartment with you. When Karla talked to Billy in her smooth, convincing way that she is so adept at during her mania, this time Billy saw through it. He told her he wouldn't let her move in. Karla was shocked and angry, but after awhile she rationalized the reason saying that it was because of Billy's girlfriend. Karla clearly had no concept of planning a functional future. Her friends in Stillwater that were very hurt and scared by her recent episode are in no position to take her in. Sadly, she's losing friends and she doesn't even know it. It's ironic that all she wants to do is "go back and be with her people, because they will understand," when the three people that love her the most and are willing to do anything to help are all right here in the same city she is now.

- Dad came over in the evening and joined Karla and me for dinner at Seamus McDaniel's, an Irish pub near my house. We had a nice dinner, but I could tell the mania seemed to be intensifying after a calm day. She was very excitable at dinner, often changed her mind about what to order, and the subsequent salad she ordered, and demanded that we buy her cigarettes "right now" after the meal concluded. Karla again had no concept of keeping her own money. During the dinner (unknown to Karla), I received a call from Lonnie just wanting to check in. I went outside and talked to him briefly, informing him that Karla was doing better and thanking him for his continued support. He is truly on board with doing anything we think is best for Karla.

- We returned home from dinner and Karla was becoming more manic. I think it was a case of sensory overload from the restaurant and being out in new surroundings. Her mind began thinking even more, and she could not control it. Though she had told me earlier in the day she wouldn't make any more long distance phone calls at my house (not that I really cared), she told dad that she wanted to call Justin. As her mania increased, she became belligerent and upset when we told her it would be better not to make the phone call. We had good reason to think this. One of Karla's revelations last night was her fear of the Internet. Two days ago, she sent a very strange e-mail to every person in her address book (friends, relatives, professors, etc.) saying she was back from a brief lovely hiatus. Hardly lovely, if you ask me. She received some responses, including a horrible message from an abusive ex-boyfriend. She began to have many delusions that people would sabotage her life via the computer. Because of this, she asked me to delete that message from her account and to monitor her e-mails over the next couple days. She also said she wanted me to read some of the e-mails that Justin had written her. She told me that she wasn't exactly sure how to understand him right now. She said she felt a bond with him, but she also said it seemed as if he was not being clear with her. He had been somewhat evasive. I checked Karla's e-mail earlier in the day, deleted the ex-boyfriend's message, and blocked his email address so she would never receive another message from him. I felt bad reading Karla's mail, but I read a couple that were very supportive (from Lonnie, Margi, Norah). I then read the e-mails Justin had written, at Karla's request. A couple e-mails were written prior to the major manic stage. I know that she had described him as eccentric and, since I met him that was my impression, too. Whether it was an attempt at poetry or something I didn't know, but it sure didn't make sense to the normal person reading it. I could see where even Karla might be confused. However, I didn't see anything inherently harmful about them, just somewhat confusing, and Karla didn't need this kind of message right now.

• As Karla smoked outside and argued with my dad about the use of the phone, I quickly checked her e-mail again. She just received an e-mail from Justin. It angered and frightened me more than anything. The subject of the message was, "top secret." The content simply said, "shhhh, don't tell your family, I am a secret agent who wants to talk to you. Call me and I will explain." I've never been angrier with an individual. Here I am trying to do everything in my power to save my sister's life and this guy, who I made a very difficult phone call to a couple days earlier asking for his help and patience in corresponding with Karla, is trying to turn this into a game of FBI with my sister. Whether it was his untimely attempt at humor, it certainly wasn't funny. And for him to not even respect me enough to remove himself from the situation until Karla was thinking clearly was completely selfish and pompous. It was clear to me at this time that Justin had no idea what bipolar meant and the little trust I had in him was now gone. If I were him and a girl that I liked was going through a bad enough time in which family members actually called me asking for help, I certainly would have approached it in a different way. I would have first done my research on the illness, stayed in contact with the family as I told him to do to monitor her progress, and realized that if my relationship with the girl was meant to be, it would eventually happen. Justin did none of these things. Rather, he attempted to add to the delusional thinking that was plaguing Karla right now by trivializing her illness into a mystery game. And even if he did not knowingly do this, it's not exactly what I would call a good friend. I deleted the message, but saved the text and I will share it with Karla later. Though a small part of me feels bad about deleting it, I was only doing what Karla asked me to do—monitor her e-mail for anything potentially harmful. I also deleted a few spam e-mails, which Karla had earlier said were direct messages meant for her by the gods of the Internet. Well, the gods must like me a lot because if she only knew the amount of those I received in a day, she would probably tell me I am doomed.

- I suggested Karla call Lonnie rather than Justin and she agreed to that. She seemed much happier and relaxed after they talked. Exactly what she needed. Late that night I stayed up until 3:00 a.m. writing long e-mails to Lonnie and Margi, people that I knew Karla would be contacting in the next few days. Margi is a dear cousin, fifteen years older, whom Karla re-connected with at a wedding in early July. It was important to update them on the situation and thank them for their love and support. Karla was still awake when I finished and said she couldn't sleep. Her mind was racing. It was going to be a long night for her and I was worried. But I had to get some sleep. I had an important interview the next day for a potential out-of-town project that could be starting soon. I needed to be as ready as four hours of sleep could make me.

Wednesday Aug. 14

- Wednesday started early for both of us. At 8:00 a.m., Karla had already been sitting on the front porch for over an hour talking with neighbors and passers-by on my street. She was smoking and frantically making string bracelets, a hobby which she started yesterday during her mania. She seemed in a good mood and very happy—and also still clearly manic. She said she just couldn't sleep. I suspect maybe she got a couple hours.

- The day was relatively uneventful compared to the last few. I was involved with work and had my interview for a project in Milwaukee. It went well and I was assigned to start on the project the following Monday. It struck me how the timing of Karla's episode was almost meant to be with my work schedule. Had I been involved in the middle of a project out of town, it scares me to think what might have happened to her and where she would have gone. God was with us. I'm convinced that having her in a calm environment with only me was a good thing for her. I told her during the day that one of the reasons I wanted to limit her phone calls was not to try to rule her life, but more to limit her amount of stimulus with other surroundings. My theory was that this would decrease the mania. She agreed with this and after she understood, admitted that I was only trying to help her. The connection we had the past few days has been very strong, though I'd much rather connect to the functional Karla.

- Karla's day consisted of a lot of CNN watching, sitting on the porch, drinking coffee, and pacing throughout my house. Every now and then she would go into stories about gods and goddesses and inner spirituality—all signs that the mania was still there. And it's not like you can disagree with her when she tells these stories or she will become belligerent and frustrated.

- My roommate, John, came home from work in mid-afternoon. I kept him updated on Karla's events the past week, and he was a strong source of support for me. This was the first time he had seen her. I was curious to get his impression and left him alone with Karla for awhile. She explained to him the gods and goddesses and then tried to analyze what type of astrological sign and animal he was. She was so convinced she would know his sign, it was pretty funny when it took her to the 12th month to guess correctly. John could clearly tell that Karla was not completely in reality, but she was relatively calm and he was good with her. Basically, he just had to listen, as everyone does, when Karla starts speaking endlessly during her mania.

- Karla said for the past two days that she wanted to clean my screened-in porch. Finally, late in the afternoon she does it. And she did a great job. When she gets focused on a task, the results are usually remarkable. I even suggest the possibility of getting a job as a housekeeper in Stillwater. She's excited about the idea and says that will be perfect. She'll look into it next week. I keep thinking about how we can help her in the next few days to remain focused. It's a comforting feeling that she will see her doctor tomorrow in Stillwater, and as of now, the plan is for her to enroll in classes for the semester. The structure and day-to-day life is truly the only thing that will bring Karla back to reality. Any outside influences or unordinary visitors would probably be negative influences, in my opinion.

- The evening approaches and my dad arrives at my house to take Karla to the airport for the trip to Tulsa. He has agreed to take off work to go with her to help get her settled during the next few days. Mom wants to come too but school was starting soon, and she has a lot of meetings scheduled. Karla is very excited about dad going with her and is very happy he will be there to help her. As it gets closer to Karla's time to leave my house, I create another PowerPoint printout outlining all the things to do in Stillwater the next few days. Essentially, they are basic things—find a single apartment, get a phone, subscribe to a newspaper, get financial aid, meet with her psychiatrist, etc. It is somewhat amazing to me that I would even have to write this down for her, but I have no problem doing it and she loves the printout. I include our picture on it as well.

- Before Karla leaves, she sets aside a few of her string bracelets she was frantically making. She tells me to choose one and I could have it. I pick one that's red and gold and I put it around my ankle. I've worn it every day since, and it's my constant reminder of the sister I love and the illness that challenges all of us. I don't plan to take it off. It's become a part of me, and I want it to stay that way.

- I drive Karla and dad to the airport. My thoughts are many, mostly just hope for the next few days, but for the first time in the past week, I have confidence that Karla is getting better and that she's ready to get through this. She knows she has to take her medication daily and she promises me she will. I believe her and I trust her as I always have.

- Dad and Karla arrive in Stillwater on Wednesday night and they stay in a hotel. Karla is excited to be back in her surroundings, is still a bit manic, but knows that tomorrow is an important day.

Thursday, Aug. 15

- I'm now out of the direct picture and it's both a good and scary feeling. I want to be with her so much, but physically, emotionally, and mentally I am just drained. I reflect a lot on the past few days and know that this experience is a turning point in my life. Never before did I focus on a particular time period or event as I did in the past three weeks.

- I continue to do more research on bipolar and have actually started some e-mail conversations with other bipolar people across the country who read my story about Karla through an MTV chat room. I exchange e-mails with three different people who were struggling with possible bipolar illness and who tell me that they now feel a lot better about what they need to do to get help. In my mind, I feel that I have some valuable experience, and it's a good feeling to be able to help others. I could see myself getting into some type of bipolar support role in the future.

7

Mania Unchecked

Kevin's chronology continues, but since I spent the next ten days in Stillwater with Karla, I will continue the story from my perspective. Chapter 8 returns to Kevin's account and the two months following my trip to Stillwater.

Karla and I flew to Tulsa on Wednesday, August 14, met Mark and Paddy Swiney at the airport, and they took us to Karla's 1990 Honda Accord. In the middle of a hot, humid Oklahoma August, she and I drove the ninety miles to Stillwater in her car that had a broken air conditioner and needed some other undetermined repairs somewhere. I drove because I didn't trust her mania or the car, and she didn't object because her mind and her mostly one-sided conversations raced from one topic to another, only to collide with another new topic. Driving would interfere with her frantic stories. I was able to keep up with her conversations, and we actually enjoyed the time in the car together, though I was constantly on edge, not knowing what she might do next. By this time, I didn't really care what she said, but I was very concerned about what she might do.

I spent ten days with her. Her unchecked mania rambled through the hours, taking everyone and everything with her. It was the most exasperating and exhausting time of my life. She was cheery and delightful, but extremely impulsive, with a stream of frantic consciousness and endless energy. My goals were to get her meds adjusted (but her doctor was on vacation), find a suitable apartment, move from the house she shared with Art and Marie, buy what she needed, get her enrolled in school (she had missed some deadlines and there were complications with her student loan), and keep her safe. This final task was the most challenging—she was very friendly with everyone, especially men.

The Best Western we stayed in was being renovated. A crew of bricklayers was replacing the outside façade of the hotel, using a scaffold to reach the upper floors. While I was checking in, Karla was checking out the crew. She immediately began a conversation with the foreman who was on the ground talking with the men on the scaffold. When I corralled her to go to our room, she said good-bye to the foreman like he was her best friend and had known him for years. I was physically tired but emotionally and mentally alert. In her state of mind, she was easy prey for anyone who was even slightly interested in pursuing a "relationship" with a beautiful, charming twenty-six-year-old woman. I was determined to protect her from anyone in that category—and from herself. I didn't know how long I would have to watch her in order to feel comfortable with leaving her alone again, but I did know that she needed more medication before I could relax my twenty-four hour a day vigil. For the next five days, she maintained a casual and friendly relationship with the bricklayers. I remained watchful.

A Night on the Town

One night I went with her to Stonewalls, her favorite bar, a sociable place that attracted the English lit, philosophical crowd who genuinely enjoyed their animated discussions about political, social, and literary issues and ideas. She fit right in, and that night, she was fitting in all over the bar. I kept my eye on her as she flitted and flirted, even as I drank a beer and had a quiet conversation with some of her friends. By 1:00 a.m., I was very tired when she was not. When her friend Michelle, agreed to bring her to the hotel, I left. As it turned out, I should have stayed at Stonewalls because I couldn't sleep anyway. By 7:00 a.m., she had not returned. I was getting frantic. I called Michelle and she said she dropped Karla off at 3:00 a.m.. My anxiety increased about three notches. I went outside and looked around for the fourth time, and there she was walking peacefully and calmly toward the hotel. She just went for a walk around the city, she said, and what was the problem?

I called Cindy Washington, a wonderful woman who was Karla's counselor. I had visited with Cindy previously and had a great deal of respect for her. And, even more importantly, so did Karla. We agreed that we could no longer wait for Karla's doctor to get back in town and agreed to meet at the emergency room of the hospital. Karla cooperated but needed some cigarettes and asked me to get her some on the way to the hospital (she had no money). I stopped at a nearby supermarket, bought her cigarettes, got back into the car, drove to the hospital, and then noticed she was barefoot. She said she threw her very good sandals out the window while I was in the store because someone else had worn them at one time and she didn't like that girl. It made no sense to me, but by then, we were near the hospital and, barefoot or not, I was determined to get her to the emergency room. Cindy arrived shortly after we got there.

When the doctor asked Karla what was the matter, she went into a long, rambling stream of consciousness which, as I recall, mentioned things like hair braids, the beauty of all things, Tapestry, the free university she was creating, and the value of not wearing shoes. After consulting briefly with Cindy and me, he gave her some Haldol and Effexor. Karla had taken these medications before, and to her, the Effexor was okay, but the Haldol brought back frightening memories of Tucumcari, New Mexico and Parkside Hospital in Tulsa. It took some effective encouragement from Cindy before Karla took both pills. We thanked Cindy for coming out on a Saturday morning to support us both. When Karla and I got back into the Honda, we knew we just turned an important corner to her recovery.

Getting Her Settled

The next few days were extremely busy. It was a good thing. It takes considerable time for the medication to reach maximum effectiveness, and her mania was by no means over. Having major tasks to complete helped divert attention from her inner life and delusional thoughts to more practical and immediate matters. But after all of the manic energy of the past few weeks and the enormous loss of sleep, she was beginning to tire out rather quickly while we tackled one task after another. Her gradual need for more rest and sleep was the most beautiful sight I could imagine. It didn't come often or quickly, but after a week of nonstop, intense vigilance, I was exhausted and badly in need of any hint of relaxation and worry-free moments.

After days of scouting, telephoning, viewing, analyzing, and rejecting one apartment after another either because it was too small, too dirty, too expensive, or in a neighborhood that seemed unsafe, we finally found one that seemed great at a reasonable price. The bonus was that the landlord was very kind and accommodating (which was verified as the next few months unfolded), and that the other renters in the apartment building seemed stable and friendly (which also was verified in time).

Karla was still very manic during this search and, frankly, she wasn't much help. Her mind and attention were on another level, interpreting all these events from some totally different perspective. At the time, I didn't know where she was coming from, but I knew it wasn't where the rest of the world was living. I was able to intervene in her reverie just enough to get her approval, sign the lease on the apartment, and be happy with the decision. Since she had no money, Fran and I made the initial payments, and I made a private, verbal deal with the landlord to watch out for her as best he could, and I promised I would stay in contact with him periodically regarding payment and any other matters that might emerge. He was a kind man.

Art and Marie supported both Karla and me. They were as helpful as possible, but they were painfully aware that they couldn't be responsible for the manic Karla. I certainly understood and sympathized with them. It took a few days and a number of trips, but with the help of some of her friends with a pickup truck, we eventually moved all her stuff to her new apartment. It didn't take long for her to mark her living space with her posters, neatness, and unique style. By this time, she had moved so often that she could transform any space into "Karla space" in a matter of a few hours, even when she was quite manic.

I remained very wary and watchful, particularly as she met and related to the people who lived in her building. Everyone was an instant friend—the same attention she gave to the bricklayers at the hotel, she now transferred to her neighbors. This attention was even more frightening now because she would be here for a longer time and could develop an on-going relationship with some of these people. I had no basis for suspecting any of them, but I was worried about what Karla might do until she was stable enough to recognize appropriate boundaries in her relationships. When she moved in, she was nowhere near that stability.

The bureaucratic complications with enrollment, which included going back and forth three times to the bursar's office regarding her student loan, were irritating but manageable. The people were nice and helpful, which took some of the frustration out of the process. Eventually, everything was in place.

Getting into the classes she needed at this late date was no simple matter. Fortunately, Karla had a good relationship with the dean of the English department, and he worked with her to adjust her schedule and her course requirements. There aren't too many English majors at Oklahoma State, so both students and professors all know each other quite well. Karla was respected by students and profs alike as a bright, energetic, and engaging student who always participated in class discussions, wrote extremely well, spoke convincingly and passionately on many topics, and was a central personality among the "in" crowd of the English department. Because her college career was interrupted by her illness, she was a senior who was older than most other students, and her added life experiences offered a perspective on the discussions that other students didn't have. In other words, she was popular as well as intelligent.

I went with her while she made the arrangements to change her classes and enroll. She was obviously "in her element." She went from office to office and classroom to classroom like she "owned" the building. At one point, she met the professor who guided the publication of the student poetry magazine and he invited her to be an editor and an officer in the English club this year. She was thrilled with the honor and looked forward to working with him and the other members of the magazine staff.

While we were there, she heard that there was a lunch being served in one of the classrooms for the faculty of the English department. She immediately assumed that she was also invited, headed for the room and dragged me along. I've been around schools enough to know that these beginning of the school year luncheons are meant for faculty only. She plowed right into the crowded room, said hello to everyone there, announced that I was her dad, and proceeded to grab a plate, and get in the potluck buffet line, jabbering all the time. It took me two seconds to know that we were not invited and some of the folks there shot us looks that told us so. Karla missed that message completely; she was chatting it up with one of the professors like they were bosom buddies and professional cohorts.

I was embarrassed but not surprised by her behavior. She was making a fool of herself (and me too), but after everything else in the past month, I figured crashing an English department party was not my primary concern. I worried about the lasting effect this intrusion might have with some of the professors and the talk it would generate among the students when the word got out—which it probably already had! I shrugged my emotional shoulders, hoped she could reestablish her good name after the mania ended, and tried to make the best of it.

Actually, I wound up talking with Dr. Andrea Koenig, one of Karla's favorite professors. Andrea taught memoir writing and was helping Karla with her memoirs. This learned, wise, and pleasant professor was very complimentary of Karla both as a student and a writer. According to Andrea, Karla could become a successful, published author. She needed to organize her material and dedicate some time to the project, but Andrea was confident that Karla had the talent to be an author. I was thrilled, because for many years, I, too, felt that Karla was publishable. Hearing confirmation of that opinion from Andrea was very encouraging. I immediately envisioned my daughter after this mania, and after the predictable, following depression, publishing her first book and me sitting in my reclining sofa reading it proudly, with a Rob Roy by my side, a gentle fire in the fireplace, and the telephone off the hook.

But then I heard Karla laugh too loudly from across the room and realized that I had to deal with the present moment and let my dreams go for the time being.

Her Senior Year

That evening when she finally fell asleep and I collapsed into my bed, I struggled with my emotions as I reviewed the day. Getting her to her senior year was a painful, eight year nightmare. Just one more year. Then she could move on, even if it meant graduate school. It would be a milestone, an accomplishment which could propel her into a future when her potential and her best qualities would blossom. It would be a time when she would be stable, truly committed to her career, get married, have children, and move through succeeding decades with the normal ups and downs of life, her illness in check with the proper medication and her counselor. I always felt that her degree would be a major catalyst to that future life. She would not be a "failure" if she didn't get it, and I wouldn't love her less. But I was convinced that her graduation meant that much to her, especially after the years of illness that prevented her from graduating sooner.

For decades, I told her that her college graduation was going to be my "third drunk." I got drunk once when I was in high school (I will share no details of this memorable event at this point!) and once in

1978 when I was determined to finish off a bottle of Christian Brothers brandy while playing Canasta at home. The bottle was bigger than I thought, but I made it and then promptly needed help to find my bed. But I planned to get drunk for a third time at her graduation as a symbol of celebration and relief.

Beginning her senior year refreshed this dream. On the other hand, the reality of her mania sabotaged my vision and painted a very different picture, one that did not include a celebratory, drinking father of the graduate. This vision depicted an endless repetition of frantic days like these past weeks, followed by many nights of her blankets becoming her silent prison once again. Dare I dream the good dream while the nightmare lurked in the shadows? I finally fell asleep, but I woke often.

There was another area that concerned me. Karla was always interested in paranormal or paranatural phenomena. Things like intuitive communication, tarot cards, astrology, horoscopes, psychic experiences, etc. attracted her. These were not just casual, interesting theories to her, like they are with millions of people; she placed substantial credence in them. This credence expanded when she was manic to such an extent that more rational, observable insights were ignored or minimized.

It always puzzled me how someone with her mind and her amazing ability to think critically could place so much validity in these paranormal theories. On the one hand, she insisted on proof, on demonstrating rational thinking, on questioning opinions, theories, and suppositions. That's one reason why she enjoyed college so much—to learn about and develop those critical thinking skills and methods. I was very happy to see her gain that knowledge, skill, and insight. On the other hand, she totally and uncritically accepted the claims of these paranormal theories. At times, she placed much more validity in unsubstantiated, esoteric, intuited insights than in plain, common sense, observable data. To me, that's a contradiction. I hoped she would come down much more strongly on the side of critical thinking than the paranormal. And when she was manic, the paranormal quickly became fertile ground for outright delusions.

She and I talked about this after I had been in Stillwater for about a week. She was still manic, but the medication she received in the emergency room was beginning to have some minimal positive effects. We were in the car and she just described a tarot card reading she recently experienced. I responded more directly and negatively than I had ever done before. By this time, I was exasperated with all her paranormal theories and beliefs.

For example, she told me that the whole time before she went to the emergency room was really about a television documentary that was being filmed. She genuinely believed that everything she did was mysteriously directed by Justin who was in Madison, Wisconsin, and that there were hidden cameras everywhere recording her life. She was the first subject of many such documentaries. Everything she said or did and everyone she met was part of this film. The bricklayers were cast members, the night at Stonewall's was part of the script, and the search for an apartment was controlled by Justin and his assistant directors. It was all done in order to attract viewers and to keep the documentary moving along and interesting. I asked if I was in the movie too, and she said "Oh sure, you were one of the main characters." I secretly hoped this phony documentary had a happy ending.

She also said that when she was really manic she could hear each instrument very distinctly as she listened to music on the car radio. She loved being manic, even though she had no connection with the real world.

I told her that I would not listen to any more of these stories and theories. I wanted to force her into some reality. I wasn't going to contribute to her mania any more, and I urged her to connect with my world. I went so far as to tell her that I was her "drill sergeant" and expected her to follow my directions. I hoped that the medication was working and that she needed specific guidance to reconnect with reality. It was a significant reversal for me; I had never been a "drill sergeant" kind of father—or person. But I thought the shock approach might be effective. Besides, I was truly frustrated.

It didn't work. In fact, her reaction to my strong-arm approach was very negative, to the extent that months later she still referred to it with anger and disappointment. I wonder if it rearranged our core relationship. It was always there—a moment when her expectations and view of me changed radically. I used it primarily as a technique to shock her into a different way of thinking, but I confess that my frustration was also a part of my drill sergeant approach. If I had a chance to do it over again, I wouldn't do it. It was a mistake and I still regret it.

A Visit to Her Psychiatrist

Karla finally saw her psychiatrist on Thursday, August 22 I believe her doctor had a private practice but was available to OSU students once or twice a week. Karla was seeing her on a somewhat regular basis, primarily in order to get whatever medication the doctor prescribed.

Karla granted me permission to sit in on this consultation. The psychiatrist was cordial to both of us, even during the initial discussion about some appointments Karla missed and the recent confusion about scheduling this appointment. There was another misunderstanding that needed clarification: Karla remembered her doctor commenting in a session in January that some bipolar patients are able to stop taking lithium. Karla applied that approach to herself. The psychiatrist insisted that, if she actually said something like that, she certainly didn't mean that it fit Karla at this time. I didn't know if Karla misunderstood in order to justify not taking the lithium, or if she was convinced that she didn't need that medication any longer. What complicates this motivation for not taking lithium is her stated attraction for at least a mild form of mania.

Whatever the motivation and however Karla arrived at the decision to eliminate the lithium doesn't change the reality that, six months later, she was in the middle of a gigantic, uncontrolled manic attack. My theory is that when her body cycled into a manic phase, she was medically unprotected, and the mania moved into a psychotic stage. From the best I can piece together from her own testimony, it was around the beginning of 2002 that she gradually reduced and then eliminated the lithium. She continued taking the Effexor which regulated the depression, but she wound up completely vulnerable to the mania. It attacked her with a fury she didn't expect or anticipate.

In any case, the psychiatrist described various lithium derivatives and substitutes, and Karla agreed to take the medication. We picked up the pills as we left the building, and I saw her take them faithfully while I was there. It appeared that she was committed to staying on them. With her medication in hand, her corresponding resolve to follow the directions, her promise to see her psychiatrist for her next scheduled appointment, and her commitment to continue her counseling with Cindy, one large, dangerous, deadly Oklahoma cloud dissolved and some sun appeared. My relief was enormous. The medication was absolutely essential for her recovery, and it now felt like things were falling into place. The road was clear, and she was on the way to a much better future.

I didn't leave Stillwater until I felt she was stable enough to make it. Her meds were working, she was focused on school, she was seeing Cindy, she had many friends to support her, and she seemed committed to getting a job. I went back home feeling that this manic episode was gradually becoming history. Besides, I needed some rest.

8

My Sister
August 22–October 16,
2002

During those difficult days in Stillwater, I called Fran and Kevin often, updating them on the unfolding events and especially on the status of Karla's mania. We were all deeply disappointed when we learned the first day that her doctor's appointment was not Thursday, August 15, but Thursday, August 22. They were five hundred miles away, but I felt their worry and frustration. We all knew that the proper medication was the essential first step toward her stability. They sympathized with me because they realized how demanding the next week was going to be and how psychotic Karla could become by then. Their understanding was an oasis of comfort in the middle of a swirling storm.

I stayed with her a few days after the doctor's appointment. I felt she was safe and becoming more balanced daily. She was excited about her classes and wanted to reestablish some relationships with friends who understandably stayed away from her while she was so manic. Most importantly, she was thinking clearly and had a plan to proceed with her life. All of the major reasons for me going there were accomplished, and it was time to get back to Fran, Kevin, and my job.

I had a warm hug and a grateful good-bye from my daughter. We both cried. But these were tears of relief, not sadness. The future finally had a future. There was hope, confidence, commitment, and a willingness to take things one day at a time. It was a cherished moment, even though we were not naïve. There were still many problems ahead, but we felt that she was gaining strength and perspective and that she could make it.

Art drove me to the airport in Tulsa. We had a long, rewarding conversation, mainly about Karla, but also about our lives, dreams, and interests. At one point, he and Karla were engaged (no date was set) but for a variety of reasons, they changed their plans. Their separation was friendly, and Art remains a friend of ours.

Kevin maintained his chronology throughout my trip to Stillwater and continued it for quite some time after I came home. We pick up his narrative after I left Stillwater.

Thursday, Aug. 22–29

- I decide to keep in contact with Karla a few times a week. We talk for a couple of short times and exchange some messages. I feel better every time I talk with her. You can tell she is starting to think clearly, and it's so different talking with her now. She is actually interested in my life, too, and for the first time in awhile, I feel as if the person I've always gone to for advice is able to help me again.

- Karla mentions briefly that Justin has come for a short visit. This is scary because as much as I've tried to get through to him, I just don't get the feeling that he really understands her mania. He doesn't seem to be a very focused guy, so I'm a bit concerned. But Karla says it's just for a few days, and I trust her, so I think everything will be okay. It is a bit strange that she might be ready to jump into another relationship so soon. She recently ended her engagement with Art, although on the first night of the cruise she was worried when "she couldn't contact the man she was going to spend the rest of her life with" when Art hadn't written in a couple days. To think that was only a few weeks ago is frightening. Rebounds often happen when a long relationship ends, and even though I know there are several guys who want to date Karla, I personally think she doesn't really need a man in her life right now. She's always been involved with someone and perhaps a little "Karla time" now would be beneficial.

Monday, Sept. 1

- After a few messages, we finally have a long conversation on Monday night. I'm in Milwaukee. It's the best talk we've had since the cruise. Karla is in a very clear state of mind. It is so refreshing not to hear the mania in her voice, and her calmness strengthens me. She's very rational. She talks about her future and, more importantly, tells me about a recent conversation with the sister of Mrs. Swiney. She tells me that she is looking into the legal possibility of me becoming her legal guardian if she is ever again in a manic episode. She asks if I would be willing to take on that responsibility. I'm touched she asked me. Of course, I'd be willing to do it. But we joke about not wanting it to ever happen again. She tells me she will look into getting all the necessary paperwork so that when I come in town next month, I can sign it. She says she will follow up with me next week via e-mail. She tells me that she has a great counselor, Cindy Washington, with whom she has made a good connection. She will continue to see her weekly. She also mentions that Justin is still there, which is a bit surprising since he was only coming for a couple of days. I ask what he's doing and she says, "just hanging out; it's all good." She says he will be leaving in midweek. I'm happy for the conversation with her and honestly feel she's close to being 100% recovered. I haven't felt this calm in the past month. I thank, God.

Friday night, Sept. 6

- I back off from contacting Karla. I feel it's better for her to contact me when she wants to, and I don't want to pressure her. I just want her to maintain a day-to-day routine. She doesn't call during the week and finally I hear from her late Friday night. I heard from my parents earlier in the week, and they told me Karla was angry with them because they wouldn't provide a plane ticket for her to fly Justin back to Madison. Of course, I couldn't blame them. The last thing Karla needs right now is to start driving all over the country with a guy with whom none of us was impressed. Karla has a tendency to get angry when she doesn't get what she wants, so she is livid with my parents, especially my dad. It amazes me that she could even be mad at him after he just spent a traumatic week helping to get her stabilized.

• I'm in St. Louis at a bar celebrating a Cardinals' victory. Normally, I wouldn't answer a long distance phone call, but I've learned throughout the past month that I never wanted to miss a call from Karla. She seems to be in good spirits, although I can sense she is bit more moody. She explains that she wants to drive fifteen hours with Justin to Wisconsin, stay there a few days and then fly back alone to Tulsa. She tells me that she has to drive Justin because he doesn't have a valid driver's license. As shocking as that is to me, I consider the source and I guess it's not too surprising. I mean, is it really that difficult to have a valid driver's license? In the past I may have bought her a ticket. But at this point, I have very few frequent flyer miles since I haven't been traveling much this year, and the few that I do have I'm saving for a trip to Madrid to visit my girlfriend Angela. Karla understands and is not angry at me. I hang up the phone and I pause for a minute, and call it another twin feeling, but I have this sensation that things just aren't right.

Tuesday, Sept. 10

• I haven't heard from her since Friday, so I call Tuesday. I can't get through. I leave a message asking her to call me. She doesn't return my call all night. I'm starting to get a bad feeling, but I just don't want to believe it. I still have faith in

Karla, and though I don't trust Justin's influence, I can't imagine she would make any harmful decisions.

Friday, Sept. 13

- I'm working at home in St. Louis. I'm in the kitchen for about fifteen minutes and come back to my computer and notice an instant message from Karla's screen name. It says, "Hey Kev, this is Justin." I'm very surprised and quickly reply. He is already offline and does not log on again all afternoon. I think about it and I get scared. There's no reason he would just be writing me out of the blue. Something is wrong and I can sense it.

- I try calling again on Friday night and again no answer. I leave a calm message, just asking Karla to call back. No response.

Saturday, Sept. 14

- I'm in the shower mid-morning on Saturday when I hear my cell phone ring. I get out, see the caller ID, and I know the reason for the call. It's Marie. My heart literally drops into my stomach. I immediately call back, and Marie informs me that Karla is manic again. She doesn't know what to do. Justin still hasn't left town. Pretty simple correlation in my opinion. She says she is all over the place with her stories. She also tells me that Karla and Justin have been doing drugs this past week. I honestly am ready to fly to Stillwater and physically harm Justin. I had given him the benefit of the doubt this whole time. Now he has completely lost my trust. How can anyone who knows anything about Karla be so blinded? Marie knows that I can get through to Karla and she asks me to call.

- After fulfilling a lunch engagement, I come home and call Karla. Again, no answer. I don't want her to know that I know she is manic, because I fear she won't call back (she hasn't all week). I make up a story about needing advice about Angela and leave that message for her. I believe that even though she's probably manic, she'll still want to tell me how I should handle my relationship with Angela. I know I'll be able to evaluate her condition thirty seconds into our conversation, and all I want is to help her in whatever way I can.

- I call Marie again. Ironically, as I'm on the phone with her, Karla calls her on the other line. I tell Marie to tell Karla it's very important I talk to her about Angela, and I will call her in a minute.

- I finally connect with Karla. I tell her my fictitious story about needing advice about Angela, and in less than one minute, Karla's talking a mile a minute. I almost can't believe it. She's extremely manic again. Her flight of ideas is rampant. She talks about Angela for less than two minutes and then gets into people as animals, earth, wind, fire philosophy and just overall unreal thoughts. She asks me what I'm doing in three weeks and invites me to come to Memphis with her for a conference. I ask what it is. She says, "Oh Kev, you have to go. It's a poetry conference and we are all just going to get real. Everyone is going." I ask what the name is, is there a Web site, how is she getting there. She says don't worry about that. It's produced by Karla Smith Enterprise and everyone will be there. It's a revival meeting. All of her soul family will be there and many other famous authors. I smile a bit at the uniqueness of this delusion and even Karla laughs a bit too. But she's still convinced it will happen. Later, I just shake my head and notice a couple of tears in my eyes as I think about it. I try to imagine what's going on in her mind. She honestly believed that she was hosting a conference and several people were coming. All logical, rational thought has left her mind. The power of this bipolar illness is truly amazing and so hard to believe.

- I know that Karla is in bad shape, very similar to how she was when we talked on our birthday. Only this time, her support group in Stillwater has dwindled. Marie and Art don't want to be involved, and I can't blame them. Karla was horrible to them during her mania. I realize that as much as I know Justin is to blame for this and as angry as I am with him, he is the only person that Karla trusts right now. He is the only person that can help me. I vow to put aside my feelings about him and to stay focused on helping Karla.

- Karla passes the phone to Justin and we talk. He confirms that the reason he messaged me yesterday was because he was scared and didn't know what to do. I begin to start listing all the warning signs of the mania. He's amazed when I'm able to tell him several different things Karla has likely said and done in the past few days. But I still don't sense he really understands it. I essentially tell him all the things I told him last month about bipolar. Clearly, he didn't do any research on it or listen the first time I told him. I think to myself sarcastically, "what a great significant-other." I coach him on how to handle Karla and tell him that it is imperative Karla is on her medication as soon as possible. I tell him any kind of drugs or alcohol will impair the medication. He always tries to minimize the situation and the seriousness of it, but I can tell at least something is getting through to him. He's a bit shocked by Karla's behavior. Amazingly, he has no idea when she stopped taking her medication. He also says she's missed a lot of classes lately. He says they've just been hanging out. I stress the importance of getting to see Cindy Washington on Monday morning as soon as possible. He says he will take her there. For some reason, I just don't trust that he'll be the first one at the counseling center on Monday.

Sunday, Sept. 15

- Justin calls me again. He says she is getting worse and he's not sure what to do. I reaffirm the importance of keeping her in a calm environment, avoid travel and movement because she could end up anywhere, and make sure she goes to the health center Monday morning. It's important to decrease the stimulus to Karla's mind. I also tell him she must take her medication. That is the only thing that will help stabilize her. I know that the longer she is manic, the longer it will take for her to recover and the more danger she could be in. Bipolar episodes

generally get worse each time they happen, especially if they
happen in close succession. Trust me, I've done my home-
work. I'm really getting scared.

Monday, Sept. 16

- At 6:30 a.m. before I fly to Milwaukee, I call the OSU student
  health center and leave a message for Cindy Washington. I
  arrive at work mid-morning and finally, Cindy and I connect.
  I was hoping that Justin would live up to his promise and
  make sure Karla saw Cindy first thing in the morning. He
  didn't. It's my first time talking with her, and she was unaware
  of Karla's latest episode. We talk for almost an hour. She really
  appreciates the background I give her about the situation and
  Karla in general. She certainly reaffirms that she never suggested that Karla stop taking her medication, a claim Karla
  made when we talked on Saturday. Cindy agrees that I have
  taken all the right measures, and we have a common understanding on how to treat Karla when she is manic. She says she
  has patients scheduled all day but will see or talk to Karla if
  she calls. I will do everything I can to contact her and tell her
  to see Cindy as soon as possible. I can understand why Karla
  likes her. She's wonderful and I trust her to help Karla. Oh,
  and by the way, people at work are starting to wonder why I'm
  never at my desk.

- I try desperately to get ahold of Justin and Karla. There is no
  answer. I leave two messages. I can't believe they are not there.

- Around 3:00 p.m., Justin finally calls. He informs me that
  they are at Greenleaf State Park in the Tulsa area. I nearly
  drop the phone. Once again, he hasn't listened to anything
  I've said. He certainly didn't take her to see Cindy first thing
  Monday morning as we discussed over the weekend. He's calling because he's scared, and he thinks Karla is getting worse.
  Well obviously, genius, she's traveling to some state park, has
  a lot of stimulus from different surroundings, is talking about
  spiritual revivals, and certainly is not in reality. I wonder to

myself if Justin is more manic than Karla. He also tells me that Karla and he had a "spiritual marriage" at the park yesterday, but he's concerned because she is really thinking they are married. He assures me they are not. Nothing legal, no minister, just them talking. Let me rephrase that. Justin talking to the manic Karla who certainly isn't thinking rationally. What in the heck is a spiritual marriage, anyway, I think to myself. I mean hello, it's not like I've gotten many invites to spiritual weddings lately. And the thought that he would even discuss anything of this nature with someone who is clearly manic and in need of stabilization is the most selfish, asinine, stupid thing I've ever heard. Though I have all these thoughts, I am calm with Justin and maintain a good relationship with him. I urge him to get to Cindy as soon as possible before the end of the day. He understands and agrees and says he's glad we were able to talk.

• Around 6:30 p.m., I get a random call from an Oklahoma phone number. It's Michelle Dunn, a student and friend of Karla's from the OSU English department. I never met her or even talked with her. She's calling to tell me that Karla is in bad shape. She is "extremely manic" and Michelle is very worried. She's calling me because she was told I was her legal guardian and I could decide if she needed treatment. Michelle thinks Karla should be hospitalized immediately for an extended period of time. She explains that Karla waltzed into the English department and proclaimed to everyone that she got married yesterday. Every one who heard her couldn't believe it. They could tell there was something very wrong with her. Michelle knew what was going on because she too is bipolar. Karla then skipped all her classes for the day and went to the park with Michelle. I explain to Michelle that I have been involved all day, and we discuss what to do if Karla calls her. Michelle tells me Karla has missed a lot of classes in the past two weeks. Again, in my mind, another result of Justin being there. Michelle seems levelheaded about the situation and understands the illness. That is comforting. She says she will do anything to help and will let me know if she hears from Karla. We will keep in contact, and I think she will be a good influence on Karla.

- As I go to bed late that night, I can't sleep at all. The fear I have is intense. I picture Karla in a state park with a potentially abusive guy who clearly has no idea how to handle this situation. I picture her getting lost in the park and possibly missing forever. It's horrifying. I'm alone in Milwaukee. It's one of the worst nights of my life. I even think about how I will confront Justin if Karla is permanently harmed or even dies. I'm not a vengeful person by nature, but I am tonight.

- I find out later that this was Karla's most tumultuous night. It's ironic that I had the same twin-like feelings again. When she attempted suicide four years ago, I had trouble sleeping the night before I found out about the attempt. I had known nothing of her condition that night; I just felt a strange concern for her. God works in mysterious ways.

Tuesday, Sept. 17

- I'm at work and it's difficult to focus. I'm anxiously awaiting news from Karla, and I hear nothing all day. I contemplate telling my manager the situation I'm in but decide against it. It's just too soon in the project, he doesn't know me well, and I can't jeopardize this role.

- At 7:00 p.m., I leave work for a planned dinner at my aunt and uncle's home, Pat and Jack Herrington in Milwaukee. As I'm driving there, I finally get a call from Justin. His story is extremely sketchy, he's very difficult to understand, but the end result is that Karla is once again at the Tulsa Crisis Center, admitted through the emergency room. Justin knows very little about what is going on because the nurses and doctors won't tell him anything since he's not the legal guardian. He asks me to call. He will stay at Lonnie's for tonight.

- I arrive at Pat and Jack's, a house that I haven't been in for a few years, and I immediately ask to use their phone. I have to find out about Karla and understand what is going on.

- I call Tulsa Crisis Center, claim I am the legal guardian (a bit of a stretch in truth, but Karla gave me a verbal agreement, and I had to help her). I speak with the on-call doctor, Dr. Drummond. She had very little background on Karla. We discuss a lot. She is very thankful for our conversation. I tell her what meds to avoid, and we agree that Tryleptol and Effexor are probably best for Karla. We talk for over thirty minutes. Without this phone call, I'm convinced that the care Karla would receive at the treatment center would be inadequate. She could have been in serious danger. It's almost as if doctors give special care to those patients who have concerned families. She gives me a better feel for Tulsa Crisis Center, and I'm not as worried about Karla's safety. I will be in contact. Karla has finally slept after taking Haldol.

- The details of how Karla was admitted to Tulsa Crisis Center also become clearer. Apparently, she went to the chapel at St. John's Hospital barefoot, and a security guard approached her. He could tell she was not thinking clearly. He escorted her to the emergency room where she voluntarily admitted herself. This story is still incomplete to me, but Justin sure isn't much help with the details. Actually, he's not much help with anything except helping make my sister more manic.

- I call Lonnie and update him. We agree that I will keep in touch with Karla and Justin, and the Crisis Center might be the best place for Karla now. He continues to be so loving, caring, concerned, and helpful. We will be in touch.

- Pat and Jack are wonderful. As I tell them the whole story of the past months, I break down. I just can't believe we are going through this all over again—and just a month ago everything was fine. Their comfort reaffirms the importance and closeness of family in me. It couldn't have come at a more perfect time. I needed them that night, and we shared a beautiful dinner.

- I update mom and dad driving home from Pat and Jack's late at night. They had no idea of any of the past few days' events, and honestly, I just haven't had time to update them. They are very scared and will try to contact Tulsa Crisis Center.

Wednesday, Sept. 18

- I call Cindy Washington at OSU to tell her where Karla is. She's very concerned but grateful for the call. She said Karla seemed ready to be helped when she talked to her late Monday afternoon, but obviously her mania increased tremendously since then. I ask to talk to some of the teachers. I'm thinking long term, and if Karla doesn't have school this semester, it will be dangerous for her if she is doing nothing. Karla's long-term health and success is all that matters to me. Cindy and I agree that Karla's best place right now is Tulsa Crisis Center, and she should be there as long as she needs to become stabilized. I question this a bit because I know Karla has told me she doesn't like hospital stays, but if she is willing to accept it, then I think it's fine.

- Justin calls me in the afternoon. We have a good talk about the importance of Karla's meds. I guess part of this is starting to sink in. He reaffirms they are definitely not married. I can tell he is overwhelmed with this situation. Still talking so quickly. I suspect he's under the influence of some drug and he's difficult to understand. He always seems grateful for our conversations.

- Michelle Dunn, my parents, and Lonnie all call me Wednesday night wanting updates. Lonnie is ready to help however he can. I talk to one nurse at the Crisis Center who says Karla is taking her meds, but is still very manic. She's difficult to control, but they are paying special attention to her. I thank her for all they are doing.

Thursday, Sept. 19

- I receive a call from Lonnie. He tells me that Karla has contacted McKenna, a friend in Tulsa whom I've never met, and McKenna is going to visit Karla tonight during visiting hours. Lonnie has not yet talked with Karla. He gives me McKenna's phone number and suggests I call her before she visits Karla.

- I'm in the airport ready to fly back to St. Louis when I reach McKenna. We have a lengthy conversation as I bring her up to speed on the events of the past month. She seems caring and understanding and willing to help. She says she'll do anything for Karla since Karla was there for her last year when she was manic. McKenna obviously understands the illness well and the cycle Karla is in right now. I tell her about Justin and I'm curious to get her opinion of him. McKenna and Justin will visit Karla together.

- McKenna calls me back late Thursday night after seeing Karla and Justin. She says Karla seems very drugged and euphoric. She is certainly not herself and is still not even close to reality. The doctors and nurses I've talked with have said that she needed strong medication, and she has been receptive to taking them. McKenna will continue talking with and visiting Karla. It's good that Karla has someone looking out for her long-term interests. McKenna also tells me her initial impression of Justin. She does not like him, he seems "swarthy" she says. There's something about him she doesn't trust. The more I think about it, I think it's time Justin gets away from this situation for awhile. No one has spoken positively about him.

Friday, Sept. 20

- My day starts at 6:30 a.m. with a call from Lonnie. He's so willing to help and concerned about Karla. He tells me that Justin has been staying at Karla's apartment the past two days with her car, keys, bank card, and all her possessions. This frustrates me a bit because Justin is not family, he has no money, and if he is spending the little that Karla has, I know that will have long-term ramifications. Lonnie, who is open and accepting of everyone, is now clearly seeing the negative influence Justin has on Karla. He says that he will do anything our family says if it will help remove Justin from the situation. I give Justin more of the benefit of the doubt and presume he will leave town shortly. Lonnie says he will confront Justin, if necessary.

- I'm working from home in St. Louis, although I get very little work done. I spend my whole morning talking about Karla. As I'm online, Justin sends me an instant message from Karla's computer. We have a very lengthy conversation and for the first time in this whole chain of events, I challenge Justin on his purpose for being there. Our conversation culminates with my asking him to leave for the short term because love will see them through if it is meant to be. He is his usual noncommittal self and says he will get back to me about leaving. It's clear this guy is way over his head.

- I update mom and dad via e-mail of the happenings of the past two days. I've kept them in the loop throughout. They've done everything they could to contact Karla and Tulsa Crisis Center. They are always there for Karla. Mom has written her a beautiful letter and is even considering flying to Tulsa for one day tomorrow so she can see Karla during visiting hours.

- In between work and everything I'm dealing with now, I try calling the patient pay phone at the hospital several times to get through to Karla. Each time it is busy. Twenty-five patients share one phone. It's so frustrating because I just want to hear her voice and know she is okay.

- Angela arrives from Spain for a weekend visit on Friday night. Of course, she has been aware of all the happenings with my sister. And she has been wonderful about helping me. It amazes me how her input and understanding of the situation is so clear and logical. Though I'd rather not spend the entire weekend focused on this situation, I know it will come up several times. It's too much a part of my life right now, and so is she.

Saturday, Sept. 21

- Mom does decide to fly to Tulsa for the day and night. She will visit Karla during visiting hours. She will also talk with Justin about stepping aside for awhile. She's just being a mother trying to help her only daughter who is not well right now.

- I talk with David, the head counselor supervising Karla right now. He's very helpful and very good. He agrees that Justin should be away from Karla now, especially if he has a history of drug abuse. He also tells me bluntly that Karla is undoubtedly his biggest challenge. She refuses to follow rules and has even made sexual advances toward some of the men. A common trait of women who are bipolar is an increased sex drive. He will watch her closely but doesn't expect her to be released at her court hearing on Monday.

- I call mom after her visit with Karla to get an update. She said it was overall very good and she's glad she went. Karla cried when she saw her and cried when they discussed her letter. Mentally, mom said Karla was getting better but wasn't close to normal. Her mood swings and flight of ideas were still there. Mom also confronted Justin in the parking lot as they left the hospital. She's amazed at his lack of dedication, drive, and complete disregard for anything he's done wrong.

- Finally, after several more tries, I get through on the pay phone to Karla. I'm just happy to hear her voice, but unfortunately she's still very manic and she starts off very angry. She talks for 90% of the conversation. It's somewhat hard to take as she berates me and attacks me for not accepting Justin, especially after all I've done to help her, but I don't let it affect me too much. All I care about is long term and Karla's health and success. Karla then becomes more pleasant on the phone and we actually joke some, laugh a bit more, and it's almost like we are fine. She says she still wants to fill out the legal guardian paperwork when I am in town Oct. 19. I mention to her the possibility of being my date at Michael and Robyn's wedding. She's very excited about it and would love to go. I hope she can.

- McKenna calls me a couple of times during the day. She is much more adamant about wanting to remove Justin from the situation. She can't believe he is just living in her apartment. We all know that Karla has told him to stay, but any rational guy would at least see the problem here and be willing to listen to other people. It's clear Karla has full control of this relationship, as she often does in her relationships. Karla is best at a relationship when she has a challenge. In my mind, Justin is not a challenge; the challenge is her desire to prove to everyone that she will be with him. McKenna and Lonnie again assert their willingness to make Justin leave her apartment.

- There's no doubt in my mind that Justin has changed for the better as a result of this situation. There's no doubt he is in love with Karla, just like many other guys have fallen in love with her. There's also no doubt that his sitting around waiting, doing nothing, is also not helping anything. I agree with Lonnie and McKenna that it's time for him to leave. They will go there tonight and confront him. It's time to take some action.

Sunday, Sept. 22

- I receive an early morning e-mail from Dad. It's the most angry I've ever seen him. He hasn't slept much all night. His feelings towards Justin are mounting, and he realizes that Karla likely would not be where she is now had it not been for Justin's influence. Sadly, Karla would never look at it like this, but as a father who loves his children more than anything else, the worst thing any outsider could do is harm his children. He does not take this lightly and wants Justin completely removed from the situation. I realize this will not happen as only Karla can make that decision, but I certainly don't blame him.

- I receive an e-mail from Lonnie in mid-morning. It's the best news I've gotten in awhile. Justin was very cooperative in agreeing to leave the apartment, and Lonnie has secured Karla's car and keys. I'm not exactly sure of all the events of the night, but I'm glad they were there to help us. I would have done the same thing if I were in town.

- Late in the afternoon, I receive a surprising phone call from Justin. He's at a pay phone in Stillwater. At first he's angry, questioning why I had Lonnie and McKenna ask him to leave. He says they threatened legal action if he didn't leave. I clarified that I was never even considering getting the law involved with this. I do however for the first time feel like it's time for him to understand. He questions why I wanted him to leave and my anger for this entire situation finally reaches a boiling point. I reel off several facts about his involvement with Karla:

  - Eighty percent of the time you have known Karla, she has not been stable.

  - I talked with you for the first time on Aug. 10 and explained Karla's condition. She is in an extreme manic state. I asked you to keep your distance for awhile.

  - Two days after I talk to you, you send Karla an e-mail saying you are a secret agent and not to listen to her family. You completely disrespected me.

  - Karla has been stable for over three years without your influence.

  - You came to visit Karla "for the week" in late August. Four weeks later, you are still there.

  - You obviously don't have a job or any income right now.

  - You subjected Karla to several drugs (marijuana, shrooms, alcohol, and probably others) during your time in Stillwater.

- I warned you about Karla's need for medication, and you blatantly disregarded it until it was too late.

- You knew Karla was extremely manic, and you still discussed major topics such as marriage and the future. This makes no sense.

- You are not the first person that Karla has said she will marry. In fact, the list is probably close to ten.

- You have been living off Karla's financial aid money since your money ran out a couple weeks ago.

- You allowed a manic Karla to walk around the streets with no shoes on.

- You have told Karla not to listen to her family members.

- Every person who has met you senses an aura of dishonesty about you. Every medical professional I've talked to said you should stay out of the picture.

- You came to Stillwater without even researching anything about bipolar symptoms, knowing that Karla had just suffered a manic episode.

- If your love for Karla is true and genuine, it will survive some time apart.

- You are putting your own interests ahead of Karla's.

- Justin listens attentively. He even agrees and says he understands. He says, "I never really thought of it like that before." We close on good terms and he thanks me for the conversation. He says that he will leave town on Monday or Tuesday. I feel better getting it all off my chest, and I now have hope that he will remove himself from the situation.

- I try calling Karla all night but cannot get through. Angela is worried about me and the time I've spent with this, but again she is a wonderful support to me and knows the right thing to say.

Monday, Sept. 23

- I land in Milwaukee and again try calling Justin at the pay phone he called me from earlier. I can't get through. I want to know what time the court hearing is? I receive a call from Amanda, the court dispatcher, around 3:00 in the afternoon. They just had the hearing. Karla is not being released; rather she is going into inpatient. Amanda tells me that Karla did not seem upset with the decision. Inpatient will likely last a week at the least. She gives me the name of the counselor who will work with Karla, a woman named Nancy. I feel good about this decision because Karla still clearly has some mania, and I'd rather her be 100% when she leaves to avoid another relapse. I also feel good because I know this should mean Justin will certainly leave town as he promised.

- Dad calls me wanting to know the status of the hearing. He didn't know it because Karla removed mom and dad from all of the documents since they have been insisting that Justin leave town. They cannot find out about her. This saddens me greatly as they have only been trying to help. Again, Karla has no idea that they have truly helped save her life.

- Monday afternoon. McKenna calls to inform me of the same news. She was at the court hearing. She said Karla seemed content. She has a different spin on things, however, and says that Karla is convinced she will be released from inpatient tomorrow. She adds that Karla is getting mad at her for not giving Justin her keys. I can tell McKenna is getting frustrated. I feel bad that she is in the middle.

- Monday night. Marie calls me from Stillwater. She's concerned because she hasn't heard from Karla and wants an update. She says that Art talked to Karla earlier today, and Karla said she is coming home tomorrow. Art expressed concerns that Karla did not sound right when they talked. She talked very quickly and gave orders. It was clear she was still manic. Art will attempt to stop in to see her tomorrow. I will keep Marie and Art updated.

- I call and talk to a nurse on Monday night. Karla has been somewhat difficult to maintain, and the nurse would be surprised if she left tomorrow. I finally get through to the pay phone at 10:15. However, a staff member answers and will not allow Karla to come to the phone. Phone hours end at 10:00. I have a lot of trouble sleeping that night.

Tuesday, Sept. 24

- I sneak out of work for awhile and call Nancy. I mainly want to give them some background on Karla's situation. I feel as if I owe this to Karla to make sure she will get the treatment she needs. We have a good conversation. She agrees with my view of the Justin situation. I stress the importance of Karla getting back to school. She says that a Dr. Morton will be responsible for Karla and determining when she will be released. I ask her to have him call me.

- Later that afternoon, McKenna sends me a long e-mail. She's very disturbed by the situation. Justin won't leave. She let him shower at her place yesterday. Karla is very angry with her. My anger with Justin intensifies when I find out he is still in town. I can't believe he hasn't listened. I'm more angry because I know that Karla's other friends are being negatively portrayed in this by Karla, and if Justin would have just left, none of this would be happening. It is so sad and unfair. And Karla seems to have no understanding of her real situation.

- Dr. Morton calls me back. He says that Karla's mania on a scale of 1–10 is now a 4, and he's concerned by her mood swings. He says she is doing better, though, and he is considering a possible release, only because of her increasing missed time in school. He says that if Karla's teachers will penalize her if she misses more class this week, then he would consider releasing her. He asks me to find out.

- I don't attend an important meeting at work because I know I have to catch Cindy Washington before she leaves for the day. I call her. I explain the situation. She is so good and helpful.

We both have concerns if Karla is released too early, but Cindy tells me that Karla has asked her not to contact her teachers. Karla wants to do this herself. I suggest we call the English advisor and ask him his thoughts about Karla's missed classes. Likely, he has more pull with the teachers anyway. Our question is: will missing two more days of classes this week hinder Karla's attempt to graduate? Sadly, this is such an important decision because if Karla is released and has nothing on which to focus, she will likely relapse. Everyone seems to agree with this theory. Cindy will call Jules, the dean, and call me back.

- Cindy calls me back and says that Jules did not think Karla missing the remaining week of class will make the difference in her classes this semester. In the back of my mind, I've got a bad feeling Karla is in trouble. I can't imagine professors allowing someone to miss four weeks of classes. Apparently, Karla had been skipping a lot when Justin was in town, even before this recent episode.

- I call Dr. Morton. He agrees. He says that because of Karla's mood swings today, he wouldn't feel right letting her go. She just hasn't been stable long enough. He even says that he will up Karla's medication. I'm in agreement with this because I think Karla would want to get out as soon as possible. He suggests she remain there through the end of the week and hopefully will be back for school on Monday. All depends on how she responds.

- Tuesday around 5:00 I finally get through to the patient pay phone. Karla can only talk for two minutes. She's extremely angry and only focuses on one thing—Justin and getting her apartment keys. She says to call her back later, around 6:30. Though I'm still at work, I tell her I will. She is so bossy and angry; I'm starting to feel very helpless. She basically hangs up on me screaming.

- I get through to her on the pay phone a little after 6:30. Karla is still manic—I know exactly how she sounds when she is. All over the place in her emotions. Very angry to very nice and calm. Then she starts screaming and lecturing me on how she will make her own decisions. What frustrates me the most is Karla's complete inability and unwillingness to listen. After all I've tried to help and do the right thing, all I want to do is tell her a few things and she won't even let me speak. I tell her that I will support the Justin thing, if it's meant to be, but there is no need to rush a decision like this. Time is the true test of any relationship, and she just doesn't get it. She's so tunnel-visioned, it is scary. And it's the first time I've ever really gotten mad at her. She says that she will not speak to our parents for a few years. How insensitive could she be? They have bent over backward to help her during this time, and all she cares about is a one-month manic relationship with an unmotivated guy who doesn't have a clue on how important it is for him to leave. She makes several references to "my car, my apartment." And she says God will provide. Well, in actuality, Karla wouldn't have an apartment or a car right now had it not been for my parents, who again fronted her rent check for this month. Karla's sole anger is that Justin doesn't have a place to stay. He does though, in Wisconsin, where he lives and where he told me he would go yesterday. Karla is so blinded, I can't even get through to her. My worst fears are realized. Had Justin left yesterday and explained it to Karla, none of this would be happening. Karla would not be angry. We would not be angry, and she could probably be getting released soon. She won't listen or accept any of this. The conversation ends with her screaming at me in tears and hanging up the phone. I've never felt so abused and unappreciated in my life. I've reached my breaking point with this situation; there's nothing else I will do. It's Karla's life and I'm backing out.

• I have three remaining loose ends to tie up. First, and most importantly, I write an e-mail to Justin. He gave me his e-mail on Sunday and said he'd check it in Wisconsin. I knew exactly what would happen if he stayed in Stillwater, and of course, it happened. Karla is mad and still in the hospital. She has alienated many people except him. I go off on him and I'm so glad

I did. It brings closure to the situation for me. He only listens to a manic girl he thinks he is in love with. What a complete lack of responsibility! The best I can say about him is that he is terribly naïve and his naiveté is destructive to my sister. I don't doubt he has better intentions, and this situation has changed his character, but he lost his chance for now. I tried to defend him (especially to my parents) and to help him through this, and the one thing I ask of him, he won't do. Leave Stillwater, give it some time and he wouldn't do it. I've been a pretty good judge of character and I'm not wrong about this. I only wish Karla would see it also. She's so adamant right now, it is impossible to deal with her. Her complete disregard for authority and rules of society is disheartening. How did she become like this? I hadn't really seen it until just now. I know that to some extent it is just her and she will always be that way, but every doctor and nurse I've talked to has said Karla is a challenge because she has to do things her way. She doesn't follow rules. She has to be the exception. Perhaps, it's another symptom of her illness, but where does the bipolar begin and her personality take over? In any case, who really wants to be with a person who is always in control, always right, and always manipulative.

- I call McKenna and tell her I've had it. I suggest it's time for all of us to back away. There's only so much we can do.

- I call mom and dad to give them the update. Mom is so concerned. She has more confidence in Karla right now than I do, and she thinks Karla will come around. For the first time, I'm the one who doesn't think Karla will ever fully realize how much we all love her and how much we all did to work towards her health and happiness.

- I go to bed that night, and I finally feel a bit relieved. I'm not going to let this dominate my thoughts anymore. It has affected my job performance, my relationships, my soul, and my relationship with Karla. I feel as if I've somehow lost the battle. I learned that I can do only so much, even if I know better than she does right now what is best for her long term.

Although, I just want her to understand and be successful, only Karla can make her decisions for her life. And when her mind is made up, whether she is manic or not, you aren't going to change it. She's a very stubborn person at times, and yet she is still the most important person in my life—and I still have faith in her.

Wednesday, Sept. 25

- I receive a long voice mail on my cell phone at work from Karla. Her doctor told me he was increasing her meds, and you can tell in the message that she is not quite as manic. She talks very quickly for over two minutes and seems relatively together. She says she loves me and then orders me to tell McKenna to give her keys back. Karla wants them dropped off at the treatment center. You can sense the anger in her message. She's concerned she won't be able to get her keys when she gets out. In my mind it's a ploy to get her keys so she can give them to Justin, which I will not support. Again, had he left town like he promised, this would not be an issue.

- McKenna has written me another long e-mail, and she is near her breaking point. I am getting there as well. I call to tell her she's done enough, and I tell her to take the keys to the treatment center. However, I tell her only to make the nurses aware that the keys are there so when Karla is released only she will have them.

Thursday, Sept. 26

- Karla is released and returns to Stillwater with Justin. I don't even receive a phone call. That doesn't bother me as much because I know Karla is only focused on one thing, but I just wish she knew everything I've done to try to help her during this time. It's not my place to continue initiating contact with her now, as much as I'd like to. The ball is in her court, and if she is not willing to understand that all of my actions had one goal in mind—her long-term happiness and health—there is nothing more I can say or do that will help her.

Sunday, Sept. 29

- I leave a message for her to see how she's doing and to let her know that I will be coming to visit her the weekend of Oct. 19. All I want to do is see her. I've asked for an extra day off work and changed my flights so that I could spend time with her. As long as she is doing better, I plan to share this chronology with her. She's dominated my thoughts over the past two months; I'm so ready to just see her and know that she is okay.

Monday evening, Sept. 30

- Karla calls me late at night as I'm driving home from work in Milwaukee. She wanted to tell me about a dream she just had and we have a good conversation about life in general, the meaning of it all, and where we fit into it. For the first half of the conversation, I feel a strong connection to her, and it almost feels as if I'm talking to the sister I know. Then she tells me how it's been difficult to catch up with school. She feels behind, and some of her classmates have made a few comments about discussions they've had when Karla was in the hospital. Karla says they have made her feel bad for being gone. I know that Karla loves to be involved in all class discussions and share all her opinions vocally, so I merely suggest that she might feel better if she backs off for a few days until she and her classmates are caught up and on the same page. This sets her off. Her mood swings during our conversation were dramatic. I give her one little suggestion, and she turns it into the fact that I don't know her and don't care about her and she doesn't want my help. I'm shocked because I wasn't even trying to convince her to do anything, I was just doing what people do when they talk—try to comfort her. It was clear she was upset, but once she got mad, there was no getting through to her. She tells me she will not talk to mom and dad for a couple of years, won't come home for Thanksgiving or Christmas, and will not tell them where she is living. She says she has written an angry letter to me about everything I did wrong during her hospital stay. I should receive it soon. Karla remains angry and hangs up the phone on me in tears ... I'm shocked and am nearly sick to my stomach. A perfectly wonderful conversation just turned ugly in a matter of minutes, and I wasn't even allowed to talk. My only hope is that when I visit her on Friday, Oct. 18, it will be better. She is aware I'm coming and hopefully she will be there. Sadly, I'm not so sure.

Oct. 1–10

- I have yet to receive the promised letter from Karla and attempt to call her to remind her of my visit. I cannot get through. Her phone has been disconnected. I talk briefly to Marie who informs me that Karla's car had broken down, Justin's car was stranded somewhere on the highway, and Karla has severed ties with Art and Marie—calling her a heinous bitch. I'm just struck by the complete animosity Karla now has towards so many people that truly love her. That is certainly not the Karla I know. If she would really take the time to think about everything and everyone else's perspective rather than her own, she might realize it also. She created a battle out of this, and in my mind, the sole reason for the battle is Justin. If he's out of the picture, the battle is certainly not at this level. But of course, I know Karla well enough to know that her mind will not be changed. And even though basic life necessities, such as a telephone, a car, a job are not among her priorities, it reaffirms my thoughts about Justin—he may love Karla and vice versa, but he certainly has no idea how to provide for her and give her the things that my sister deserves. Spiritual connections are nice, but they don't provide food, shelter, and basic life necessities. That is what saddens me the most.

- Lonnie and I trade e-mails a few times, and he's hurt by Karla's anger towards him. I feel bad because I put him in the middle of this situation, and it has only caused him stress and disappointment. He truly loves Karla, as we all do, and he truly understands her. I promise him that I will do everything I can to calm Karla's anger towards him, and if that means that Karla is more angry towards me, so be it.

- Dad writes a beautiful letter to Karla during this time and even though Karla appreciates it, I doubt it does much to change her thoughts. She calls my parents once during the past week, and they both say her mood swings are evident. She cries on the phone. We fear a depression stage could be coming on because she says her meds haven't fully taken effect. All I want to do is talk to her and tell her I trust her, love her, have faith in her and that everything will be all right, but I have no way to get ahold of her. It's so helpless when you do everything in your power to help her, but you know all her thoughts toward you are based on anger and misunderstanding.

Sunday, Oct. 13

- So here I write, one week from my anticipated meeting with Karla, yet not even knowing if I will see her. And more importantly, not even knowing how she will respond. I brainstorm about what she might say to me. I wonder if she'll ask to borrow money. I hope not. It would be hard to respond to that scenario. Another reason I wanted Justin to leave was so he would not spend any of Karla's money. I know if I go back on my word on that, I will be lying to myself and I never say things I don't believe. It will be difficult to tell her no, but I only hope that she will realize that in effect I'm following all the principles that Karla stands for. Money should not cause strain on our relationship. I want her to be able to take care of herself, and she wants the same thing. And she deserves it. Only the true feelings of love, understanding, compassion, and dedication—many of which I learned directly from my sister—could help make our relationship as strong and stable as I know it can be.

Wednesday, Oct. 16

- 1:21 a.m. So I sit in bed for the 4th night/early morning in a row feverishly trying to make sure all my thoughts, feelings, and emotions have been captured in this chronology. It's been strenuous working until 10:00 p.m. every night this week at the office and then coming straight home for dinner, and a couple of hours working on the chronology. I'm glad I've done it this week, though. I had begun to lose faith in the battle here, and I had begun to not like the person that is my sister. But my review of this and additional thoughts have changed me a bit. I'm no longer willing to just throw in the towel on this. I have no regrets about what I did because I love my sister like no other, and all I want is her happiness and mine along with it. I'm struck tonight by the sad reality that I still don't know if I will see her tomorrow or even Friday. I've asked Cindy Washington to tell Karla to contact me, but she hasn't. And I still don't know how to track her down. I promised myself and I promised Karla I would share the story I had been writing with her when I saw her in October. And I firmly believe I'm a man of my promises. I pray she is still planning to meet me in the next two days because the day has been circled on my calendar and in my heart for the past two months. I just want to hand this to her, hold her for a minute, and know that she will read it. And I just want to know that everything will be okay. This marks the end of my story, and the rest of the story is for Karla to finish, and only Karla. I trust her and I trust her decisions. It's time for this to rest now and forever, and it's time for me to rest. And it's time for my mind to rest—peacefully.

Kevin's cover letter was included with his chronology:

October 16, 2002

My Dearest Twin Sister,

It's been said that life is what happens to you when you have other plans. When I last saw the true Karla as we departed our family cruise on July 13, little did I know what plans would soon be a part of my life. Life is a long, winding road with certain stops along the way that define who we are, what we believe, and where we will go. The past three months have been a defining moment in my life. And even though you were unaware, you've helped define my life and for that I will be forever grateful.

During the past few weeks, I've reflected upon you and us and this situation and I felt defeated, depressed, and angry. Yet, as I have finalized this promised chronology for you during the past week, it has had a profound effect on me. It has reaffirmed my desire to fight for our relationship.

I will not preach to you or try to change you, and these writings are not meant to do so. They are meant for you to understand me, to understand what your bipolar illness has meant to me, and to understand my love for you. I will not tell you why you need to take your medicine every day, for you already know this. I will not tell you what decisions to make in your life, for your brilliant mind can make them for yourself. I will tell you that I will support you in whatever you do, for as long as you are happy in every phase of your life, I will be happy with you.

I share this with you only out of love and hope for your wonderful future. I share it because I promised you I would, and I take pride in my promises. I told you someday I would share everything with you from my perspective because I want you to know—and you deserve to know.

As you read this, I'm sure you will feel different emotions. Perhaps you will remember some events, some events will be new to you, and some events might surprise you. You may at times feel angry about what you read, you may disagree with what I say, and you may wish you could change what happened. I expect that and it's okay. We are different people with different ideas, but even in disagreement, I ask you to please be assured of the one underlying reason I stayed up many late nights to write this—I will do anything for you. Always have, always will.

I don't share this with you to make you feel guilty for what happened or for me to appear the hero. Quite the contrary, I don't believe in heroes or pedestals. We are all one people—sharing together, growing together, and learning together. So what I give you are my emotions, my thoughts, and my perceptions. That is my gift to you. And in my mind, it is the essence of the truth of the past three months.

I love you (and this time I said it first).

Your brother always,

Kevin

9

The Cycle Ends

Kevin did meet with Karla on October 17. She was grateful for the chronology and the time and concern he put into it. They had a good visit, but she was still manic and didn't discuss details of his gift. Kevin left Stillwater with a sense of some completion but still uneasy about her condition.

After she read the whole document, she felt a need to defend Justin. It was evident that we all wanted him to leave. He didn't want to go, and Karla wanted him to stay also. She did not want to look at her behavior, illness, or how she was affecting the rest of us. Her mania blinded her, and, typical of her illness, she couldn't get beyond her own feelings to empathize with people who didn't completely agree with her.

For his part, Kevin needed to give her the chronology. It was his way of expressing his love for his twin sister—not the only way, but at this time, certainly a significant gesture. He felt that the chronology would probably be more beneficial after this manic phase and the predictable depression which would follow. At that point, he believed his record of the past three months would help her in the continuing struggle with her illness.

During the rest of October and through the first two weeks of November the mania continued. She kept a journal but it is unintelligible: page after page of graphs, drawings, shorthand notes, some text, lines and arrows going in all directions, snatches of poetry, phone numbers, lists and blank pages. It reflects how scrambled her mind was, and how manic and, at times, how psychotic, she was.

Looking through the journal now, I search again for clues to her illness, not the symptoms that show up on the pages but the causes that continue to elude me. I want to go back to October 2002, and crawl into her mind to bring some order and peace. I want to grab hold of her erratic impulses and force them into a logical sequence. I want to breathe healing chemicals into her skull and rearrange her brain cells. I want to search relentlessly through the labyrinth of her brain, hunt down the tiny, diabolical part that feeds her illness, torture that evil for a delicious second, and then blast it into permanent nothingness. I want to reconnect the healthy cells with tender stitches and soothing ointments. I want to post a permanent nurse in her brain who will immediately destroy any future bipolar intruder who might want to attack my daughter. I want to discover the real Karla, longing for her to reappear with all her dreams, gifts, instincts, and passion.

In reality, all I do is page through her disjointed journal, puzzled by visual ramblings, frustrated by scribbling, and seeking clues in a clueless world.

Thanksgiving in Stillwater

By Thanksgiving she was truly stabilizing. Her doctor changed her medication again, and she responded well. Fran and I drove to Stillwater for Thanksgiving and spent a week with her—taking care of her bills (which were completely out of control while she was manic in August, September, and October), getting her established for her meds through the state, fixing some things in her apartment, and helping her prepare for a job at Arby's. Thanksgiving dinner was turkey stir fry and cranberry sauce (one of her favorites). We had just finished hours of identifying and organizing her bills and finances, and we were truly thankful. When we left Stillwater, we felt good about the visit, what was ahead, the real possibility of her graduation the following May, and her stability.

Typical Mania

During the mania, Karla's experience of bipolar fit many of the classic symptoms of the illness. The bipolar disorder section of *Magill's Medical Guide* outlines a typical manic phase. Though she relished her "uniqueness," this generic description reads like a record of her experience:

"Prominent features of manic episodes are elation, easily aroused anger, and increased mental activity. The elation varies from unusual vigor to uninhibited enthusiasm. The anger most often takes the form of irritability. Manic patients become annoyed if other people are unable to keep up with their racing thoughts. Intellectual activity takes place with lightening speed, ideas race through the mind, speech flows with great rapidity and almost uninterruptedly, and puns alternate with caustic commentary.

"During a manic episode, patients are often excessively self-confident and lacking in self-criticism. This produces a previously unknown energy, and when that energy is combined with racing thoughts, indefatigability, and lack of inhibition, the consequences are often disastrous. During manic episodes, patients may destroy their relationships, ruin their reputations, or create financial disasters. Manic patients usually sleep very little. They rarely feel tired and are usually kept awake by the rapid flow of ideas. Sexual activity may also be increased. Manic patients often neglect to eat and may lose weight. The combination of violent activity, decreased food intake, and an inadequate amount of sleep may lead to physical exhaustion." (*Magill's Medical Guide*, Second Revised Edition, 2002, Volume 1, Salem Press, Inc., Pasadena, California, Hachensack, New Jersey, Editor-in-Chief Dawn P. Dawson, copyright 1995, 1996, 1998, 2002)

Karla experienced all these symptoms, including the reference to sex.

I hesitate to include the following section. Fran, Kevin, and I had a number of conversations about it, and we are all reluctant to discuss it publicly. Some people may judge her and think less of her. Even though we now live in a society where premartial sex is commonly accepted and expected, there remains a lingering, negative reaction, especially among some religious groups, to people who engage in sexual activity outside of marriage.

The profile of Karla as we depict her in this book is accurate but, of course, not complete. No one can capture the total picture of anyone in print. In reality, we all remain a mystery—even to ourselves. We choose to include in this account those aspects of Karla that help tell an honest story of what happened to her and to us. We debated the wisdom of describing this next part of the story, but obviously, decided it was necessary because of the impact it had on the next few months and in a desire to be honest about the major elements of her experience.

At some point during October or November when she was psychotic, Karla became pregnant. Though she learned of her pregnancy in early December, Fran and I were unaware of this reality until her visit during Christmas break. She was rather open with us about her sexual life (as she was about everything else). But it was a surprise when she told Fran and me that she was pregnant. (She told Kevin earlier.) She practiced safe sex. Her pregnancy would, of course, become a central fact of all of our lives.

Her Gifts: As She Saw Them

Around this same time she was able to write more clearly again. Her journal is much easier to read and, at times, reflects a rediscovery of her movement toward mental health. On December 7 she included a section she titled "What are my Gifts?":

"What can I use to create my world? I am aggressive and determined, with a background geared toward success. If I have not started a challenging career yet, it's because I've had a hard time—bipolar, focusing on men, on fringes, some trouble believing in myself—but these problems have plagued so many people, as Al-Anon and mental hospitals prove. But I am unique, and not unique—I have gifts, like everyone else. One difference with me is that I know well the power of the mind to determine the path. I have learned valuable skills of the mind. I know self-defeating thoughts make havoc. Another thing I have going for me is that I come from a really good place—my family, my high school, a college education, some excellent friends. I've held many various jobs, and I am fully capable of working. Work makes me feel good. I now know I can create a fully satisfying job for myself. I am more inspired than I am intimidated. I also have another gift: I work well with people in need, I always have. If I don't get a job doing this now, I surely will later. My gift is my uncanny understanding of people. My dream is to someday help people like me. Ambition is required, but I have another gift: I am not deluded by the entice-ments of unnecessary materialism or "success". Another gift: I have seen so much of life: other countries, the scales of classes, the rich varieties of love and relationships, and the reality of people in hospi-tals for mental illness. Someday someone strong, successful, and lov-ing will choose me and see my beauty and understanding. So my experience is one of my gifts. It is a rich gift. Another gift is my ability with words and writing and literature—and I'm even trained! This gift and training will be applied to a career. I might need some patience with myself in creating this career, but everybody does. Cindy told me that I would and could be a good counselor. Basically, I can apply my gifts in whatever ways I choose. That's what Chris said. He said it was about choice."

Her manic phase was finally and gradually ending. It had been five months of an extremely difficult time, and we all were exhausted but relieved when we saw signs of a transition. Her animosity toward us because of Justin lessened noticeably, her phone calls were much calmer and realistic, and she started reading again. She never men-tioned the title and I can't find it in her journal, but she was obviously reading a book that explored the feminine side of God. On the same day as the above entry (December 7), she wrote a prayer that was influenced by this book and which reveals another side of her:

"O Goddess, lead me in love and action

Remind me of my inner strength,

But also remind me that I need you to pull me out of my self destructive thoughts.

Teach me to listen to the teachers around me.

Help me to appreciate their wisdom and beauty without envying them.

Remove my blocks.

Bring me a star.

I praise you and thank you for keeping me safe and alive thus far.

I have only one day at a time.

Tomorrow, may I grow in self trust as I open myself to receiving your gifts.

Thank you for Lonnie, Jim, Michelle, my parents, Kevin, medication, safety and lessons.

Dwell in my body and mind and cleanse me of darkness and fear.

I walk hand in hand with you and exchange light with you.

Take care of me, embrace me.

Thank you, Beloved Divine, for love, for faith, for healing me."

A Move to Tulsa

A combination of factors related to school, work, her pregnancy, some relationships, and the fallout of her mania led her to move from Stillwater back to Tulsa at the beginning of December. She stayed at Lonnie's while she tried to figure things out now that the mania had passed. Her journal reflected this transition stage and listed "Things to write about" which included: "when stuff happened; hospital stays; Keystone Lake; Justin; St. John's (hospital); Behavior Health Center—both wards; Sept; Trileptal; Peace Rally; terrorists; Halloween; Risperdal; when I dropped classes; when I met Kevin; car breakdown;

phone down; mom and dad came for Thanksgiving; jobs—Arby's, bookstore, Gallegar-Iba, IHOP hostess; Village Inn in Tulsa ... "

A list like this was the beginning of her writing process. Undoubtedly, she had some ideas about how she wanted to develop each of these topics and was getting ready to put something on paper. She was clearly looking to a future that incorporated her memoir into her life, a memoir that would certainly describe the events of the previous three months from her perspective.

On December 8 and 9, she interviewed and took a test at Village Inn in Tulsa to become a waitress. She was accepted and on December 10 she started working. She was also very conscious of her pregnancy as this December 8 prayer indicates:

"My God, nourish me, feed us both.
Thank you for the light and love that surrounds me, embraces me, from friends, from Divinity.
Bless me, keep me calm and sane.
Teach me your peace.
Shelter me from fear and doubt.
Help me get a job very soon and help me get all the services I need to care for my baby.
Remind me of who I am.
Help me recognize the progress I've made mentally and emotionally.
I'm not alone because of you, the Goddess, all the angels and saints, are with me. Loving, healing me.
Bless us all. Make me strong.
I pray that you will feed us.
May a new life grow gently, healthy, blessed in love, within me.
So be it. And, Thank You."

A Change in Medication

A lot was going on at the same time. She was pregnant. She moved to Tulsa, got the job, tried to continue doing a paper for a class in Stillwater, and went to Tulsa Center for Behavioral Health. She was running out of medication, and by this time, she was recommitted to her need for meds and willingness to take them. The combination of Trileptal and Risperdal was working well, but the doctor she saw on December 9 changed her medication to 2.5 mg of Zyprexa, presumably because of Karla's pregnancy. When she told us about this change, Fran, Kevin and I expressed concern because we knew the Trileptal and Risperdal were the major reasons she was progressing so well. At this time, Fran and I were still unaware of the pregnancy. She had no real choice, and she took the Zyprexa faithfully. We hoped it would continue to protect her from her illness.

During this time also, she had to decide where she was going to live and how she intended to finish college. We talked to her on the phone often about her options and the decisions she faced. So did Kevin. She felt she couldn't live in Stillwater any more, but she desperately wanted to get her degree as soon as possible. The more we talked with her during the next few weeks, the more we feared the complications in her life, especially a devastating depression which could follow the long manic episode. She wanted to come home for Christmas, and she worked out an arrangement with Village Inn to be in Belleville for over a week, returning to work right before New Year's Day.

On December 20, she wrote another entry in her journal which described her state of mind at that point and her obvious fear of a depressive episode:

"I found out on Dec 8 that I am pregnant. The life that grows inside me could have had a better start. Like, not just the externals—a father (married to a mother and a good man), a home, built by hard work, you know—money—and stability, but more importantly, I wish I was stronger, and not bipolar. I want to be good, true, loyal, hard working. I clouded these lessons, delving into "other things". On this end of psychosis, a month after the last episode, depression waits in the wings, threatening. I feel it push in to block me from thinking about what to do. It's brought its army of little tin men—they are obsessions, poised and ready to block real thought, real action, obsessions about food and sleep. And thoughts to dismantle real thought—thoughts like I come from a different world than these people around me—Swineys—every last one of them strong and successful—so un-hiding that they can tell funny stories and be smart—so pleasant—and when I decided a few days ago that I envy them, that thought form reared its head to make it true. God love them all, they try to reach out. But I'm too far away. I am if I say I am. We all create our own distances, or nearness. I refuse to slide under the water. Mik reminded me today of what I said a long time ago: "when there's something missing, you can bet it's God".

So Dear God—
Keep me out of depression.
I can't afford it now.
I must work, wherever I live. I will work.
Do not let me have false masters—food, cigarettes, sleep.
Do not let me sabotage myself.
I've been through so much.
Work with me. Make me stronger.
Let me be embraced by your love.
Make it easier by turning my heart.
I surrender.
I want a better life.
Oh God heal me.
Make me unselfish."

Despite all her efforts and taking her medication, the depression battered her relentlessly. Her defenses—family, friends, job, school, counseling, medication, prayer, and her own determination—crumbled like bombed-out walls of a once beautiful home in a war-ravaged city, partially standing, uninhabitable, waiting ominously for the next bomb or collapsing of its own disconnected dead weight in the middle of a quiet night. Her spirit was hiding in a dark corner of a roofless, dirty, cold, half-room with the "tin men" she described cautiously but confidently surrounding her with guns raised and smiles on their gaunt faces. The depression she was all too familiar with was returning.

Her Pregnancy Revealed

Karla came home for Christmas on December 22. Kevin picked her up from the airport and, after initial hellos and hugs, they both sat on the love seat in our living room. Fran and I were sitting on the sofa perpendicular to them. It was then that she told us she was pregnant. She simply announced it, but later she said she was nervous about it. We hugged her and assured her we would do what we could to support her and the baby.

When she told us, she said she deliberately got pregnant during a manic/psychotic time and sincerely believed that this baby would be "the long-awaited Jewish Messiah." I am convinced that, at that time, she truly believed that claim. Other delusions were common during her mania and psychosis, so this delusion was one among many. It's the reason she was having a baby.

She didn't really know who the father was because there were two possibilities. She didn't want either of them to be involved in the pregnancy, birth or life of the baby. She was strongly opposed to abortion and had decided to put the baby up for adoption. Needless to say, the pregnancy complicated an already complicated life, especially as she now began to transition from mania to depression. She was, however, steadfast in her commitment to adoption.

For years, she had talked about being a mother, usually expressing a desire for anywhere from six to ten children. Her illness and college prevented her from getting married, although she had a number of marriage proposals. But being a wife and mother was definitely a major part of her plan for the future. Her pregnancy now, however, transformed those dreams into a challenging reality.

I maintained a calm exterior but internally I quickly had disconnected flashes of the next year. Over her shoulder as I hugged her I could see the two picture frames standing on the top of our entertainment center. Each frame contains the nine class photos of either Karla or Kevin as they progressed from kindergarten to high school graduation. Karla's pictures capture her growing life, its moods and phases and ultimately she emerges as a young woman. There's a story behind each picture, each year. As I held her, I felt the joys and struggles of those childhood years in one miraculous collage of feelings, hopes, and dreams. It was not a conscious reflection of all of those years; it was a sudden awareness of the whole, dynamic relationship. And now she was carrying a similar life within her, a life that will also have snapshots of growth, phases, joys, and struggles. I felt uniquely connected with Karla and with the new life who would forever have me as a grandpa. I was joyfully but fearfully stunned.

Simultaneously, I saw the difficulties of the coming year. I feared the impact the pregnancy would have on Karla's fragile psyche. I visualized Karla at six months pregnant, then eight months. I worried about the physical health of both Karla and the baby. I immediately sensed that adoption was the best approach, but I wondered if she would be able to stick to that decision as the birth approached. Her college degree dropped quickly on the priority list—at least for the next year. I envisioned her moving home with us during the pregnancy. All of these future flashes mingled with the past images in a brief collision of fear, anticipation, disappointment, excitement, joy, and turmoil. I was deeply aware that her pregnancy would forever reweave the tapestry of our family.

We then talked for a long time about what to do. We have a history of "family meetings" dating back to the twins' early grade school days. At times, these discussions were structured into "everyone shares one good thing about the day and one not so good thing". Other times, they were more spontaneous. All of those conversations came to bear on this evening's talk; we were already familiar with the style and approach each of us would take to this most serious situation. The options flowed naturally from our knowledge of each other.

The option of moving to Belleville with us had some obvious advantages but also some drawbacks. Outside of the family, she knew no one here, and Fran and I would have to go to work, leaving her alone for long periods of time. We talked about one of us quitting our job to be home with her, but that, too, was complicated. Karla considered getting a job here to keep her busy and to make a little money, but coming off the mania and with depression setting in, it didn't seem realistic that she could make a major adjustment like that. And she was clear about not being able to go back to Stillwater since so many of her relationships there were severely damaged during the past six months.

The best option seemed to be for her to remain in Tulsa, living in Madonna House, a home for unwed mothers sponsored by the Catholic Diocese of Tulsa and managed by Mag Sullivan, a friend of ours. She could also continue her education at the OSU Tulsa campus and stay with her job at Village Inn for as long as she could. Madonna House would provide an atmosphere that would help her through the pregnancy, the Village Inn job would keep her occupied, the schooling would move her closer to graduation, her Tulsa friends would support her emotionally, and she would be living in a familiar city. We would maintain a regular contact with her and visit often. That was the best plan we could figure. As it turned out, it wasn't as good a plan as we thought.

Fran called Mag who was very gracious, indicated that there was a room available for Karla, and invited her to join the little community at Madonna House. Karla accepted.

Christmas 2002

My sister Sharon, and her friend Janie, joined the four of us for our traditional, Christmas Eve, homemade pizza, and gift exchange followed by midnight Mass. The gift exchange was a ritual that included a game created by Fran and me. The game for Christmas Eve 2002 was a version of bingo that ultimately delivered cash prizes to all four of them. We had many laughs and a great time. The game was followed by exchanging gifts among all of us, one at a time, while we each ate homemade pizza and dozens of Christmas cookies that Fran bakes each year.

The highlight of the gift giving came at the end when Kevin gave Karla a cell phone with a year's contract and with the bills coming to his address. He said he had to keep in contact with his twin sister, gave her clear instructions on how to use the phone, and promised to call regularly regardless of where she was. We all cried.

On Christmas Day, we helped at noon with the annual Bishop's Dinner, an event sponsored by the diocese which provides a Christmas dinner for people who do not have that opportunity in their own homes. This was the fourth year that we helped serve the food and visit with the people. Karla truly enjoyed this event, but this year she was less spirited than usual and didn't get as involved with the people as in the past.

After the Bishop's dinner we came home. Our friend Margie, joined the four of us for our own Christmas dinner. Kevin left to join his girl friend and her family for more holiday festivities. Our family tradition for Christmas afternoon was to go to a movie, so the four of us saw *Catch Me If You Can*, a fun movie based on the real life of a man who now lives in Tulsa. Getting out of the car in the garage back home I asked Karla how she was feeling, and she told me that all she could think about was dying. We talked a little bit more in the house, but Karla just wanted to go to her bedroom and be alone. Margie left and periodically Fran or I would check on Karla. Finally, she came out of her room and began sharing with us how she was feeling.

She told us that the voices in her head insisted that she was no good, that there was no hope, that everything was messed up. She said that these voices were like demons that never stopped. She couldn't shut them up. They were very convincing. She talked for a long time. We tried to gently assure her of her goodness and beauty, and our love. She had cut her hair very short recently and she now regretted it and felt terrible about it. We reminded her that her hair was really a minor issue and that short hair was fashionable and practical. She remained inconsolable about everything.

A Dangerous Depression

I wondered if she was taking her medication which should be protecting her from deep depression. She assured us that she was taking her pills faithfully and, in fact, we saw her take them a number of times. But she was clearly moving into dangerous territory.

On December, 29 Fran flew to Tulsa with Karla to help her get settled into Madonna House and her new life. I took them to the airport, feeling somewhat confident that things were under control and that the next year would be difficult but doable. I knew that Fran would smooth out the transition problems. Little did I know that the brief hug at the airport, along with the standard "have a good trip," would be the last time I would see my daughter.

During the next few days, they made all the arrangements. Karla returned to work. They connected with Lonnie, and together they moved her stuff from Stillwater to Tulsa, storing a lot of it in the warehouse where Lonnie lived. Karla moved into Madonna House while Fran stayed with her friend and former secretary Jan Hay. I talked with them on the phone and everything was progressing according to plan, except Karla was getting sadder and sadder each day, even though she bravely made these major adjustments in her life.

On New Year's Eve day, Karla went to work in the morning. Fran and Jan visited, did a little shopping and decided to stop at Village Inn for lunch in order to be waited on by Karla. When they arrived, they couldn't find Karla. A manager informed them that she left work earlier—walked out because she said she couldn't do it anymore. No one knew where she was. She had her car, so she could have gone anywhere. Fran checked with Madonna House and she wasn't there. She had not contacted the Swineys either.

Fran then called Lonnie. Karla was there but was very depressed. By the time Fran and Jan got there, Karla was in a catatonic state—not communicating, not responsive to anyone or anything. She had written a note, which reads:

"Mom, Dad and Kevin,

I'm sorry. I just can't keep on going. You all did everything you could. Please forgive me, it is my fault. I messed everything up so bad that I just can't go on. Sorry. Love, Karla. One day before January 1, 2003.

"This was the letter I wrote this afternoon when I had a gun:

"Today I held a gun to my chest and could have shot it off but I did not have the strength. I am at a place in my life where there are three options: 1) Life (this is impossible); 2) Institution; 3) Suicide (I do not have the strength). So, 2) is my only option. Option One included staying with Lonnie, living at Madonna House, or moving back home. I cannot do any of these things.

"This is my last pack of cigarettes so don't buy me any more. I just won't smoke. As for what else, I will never eat again. I will never talk again. I will never bathe again. I am dead, as close to dead as I can get without killing myself. Give anyone any of my stuff. Tell Kevin the phone was a great idea but I don't need it. Maybe he can get his money back.

"Since this is my last communication with anyone, let me explain why it has to be this way:

Living involves doing the following:

1. supporting myself (I have never done this)

2. which means having a job (I cannot),

3. having a goal for the future (I have none—today is impossible, tomorrow will be too)

4. having faith (this is gone)

5. being close to others (I do not have this capacity any longer) because:

    a. I cannot talk

    b. I cannot be in the same room with someone who loves me

    c. I cannot communicate with those who do not know me.

"They say that attitude is everything, and 'they' are absolutely correct. I do not have control over my attitude or my mind any longer. It would be a lot simpler if I could shoot myself; I'm sorry, I just can't do it.

"When I get to the institution, I will not speak (actually my last communication with anyone will be the farewell I say to Lonnie after I write this), so give them this letter to explain. Surely there is a place somewhere where a mostly dead person can finish out her days (starvation? Or will they give me IV?) for free.

"I feel bad that there is so much of my stuff that my family or Lonnie will have to get rid of, what a headache, but that's just how it is.

"I'm sure everyone will try to make me better. As we all know, 'only I' could make me better, and that's just not possible. So say your good byes in your own ways.

"Mom, you're a good woman: a survivor. Strong, capable, faith filled, and loving. Thank you for everything. Good bye. Dad, you're the best. I hope you know. Bye. Kev, I love you so much. Be strong. Bye.

"Please tell the following people thank you and assure them of my love: the Swineys—Mama, Mr., Beth, Norah, Mik, Terry, Quin, Hugh, and Kevin. Michelle. Art. Marie.

"That's all. From now on, I'm gone. Goodbye. Karla.

"Just think of me as Grandma, with Alzheimer's. In another place. Or a cancer patient, with no hair, ready to go.

"My contacts are gone. I don't need any extra clothes. I don't need anything with me (cigarettes, phone, etc.) so just take me. All I will ever do is go to the bathroom and lie motionless.

"I know it hurts. It hurts me too. But living (Option One) hurts much more. I am ready to go to the hospital."

Fran and Jan immediately took her to the Tulsa Center for Behavioral Health. Karla remained motionless and speechless. The admitting doctor expressed surprise that Karla was on such a low dosage of Zyprexa (2.5 mg) and increased the dosage to 10 mg. immediately. The doctor indicated that Karla would be safe and that they would keep her until the additional meds took hold and she was strong enough to be released. For her part, Karla remained uncooperative and silent during the admission process. When she finally spoke the next day, she was angry and still uncooperative.

Fran called me on New Year's Eve to tell me about Karla's suicide note, her admission to Tulsa Center for Behavioral Health, and the plans for the near future. Fran was clearly exhausted, physically and emotionally. I was stunned by the events of the day. It wasn't so much total shock but rather a deafening weariness that shut down most of my senses and added hundred pounds to my body and spirit. I just sat there feeling very heavy and defeated, like a prize fighter must feel when he's knocked to the floor of the ring, not totally unconscious but still unable to get to his feet.

After going through all the details with Fran, a big question remained: how did Karla get a gun? I called Lonnie and discovered that he kept a rifle in his warehouse/apartment because of vandals who had a history of breaking into his place. It's was one of the reasons he lived there—he provided some security to his father's vending machine repair business. Karla found the gun and proposed a murder/suicide pact between them, but Lonnie refused. I asked him to get rid of the gun and he agreed to take it to his father's farm.

At midnight I was alone, and there were no "Happy New Year" festivities.

Fran stayed in Tulsa for a few more days, checking with the staff and visiting Karla when it was permitted. There wasn't much more she could do there, and we felt our daughter was now safe and just needed time, medication, and some counseling to get back onto the regimen that worked for her for three years prior to the summer of 2002. Fran was assured by the staff of the hospital that Karla was safe and that they would stay in close touch with us regarding Karla's progress and treatment as we requested. Fran flew back home.

Treatment

Karla's journal while she was in the hospital was one of the ways she processed her thoughts and feelings. She worked things out in her own mind by writing them down. Previous journals occasionally included prayers, but this journal had many of these prayers. Her written prayers reflected her spirituality as well as her emotional life from her perspective. She was never a person who simply turned everything over to God and then waited for some specific sign as an answer to her prayer. She believed in God and sought to experience that relationship, but she also believed she had to take appropriate action to change her thinking, adapt her feelings, and do what was necessary to achieve emotional balance. Her letters to God were also letters to and about herself.

Her first entry in her January, 2003, journal was one of these letters, dated 1–2–03:

"Dear God, I ask you back into my body, soul, and mind. You are my comfort because you have seen everything I've been through, and I don't have to explain ... When I was depressed before, I wrote to you and got better. Thank you for my family and Lonnie. When I am suicidal I feel Other Presences, and they are not of you. Please remove them. I know you can. I'm not as beautiful as I once was, and this hurts me, but beauty is in the soul and together we can cultivate my soul again. I welcome you with open arms. You are my salvation. Please guide my path, one minute at a time, through the people I meet and the events that happen. I promise to continue to write to you a couple times a day. I am knocking on your door, ready to receive your Light. Strengthen me and fill me with your love. Mom and dad are reasonable to hesitate on me coming home right now. There's no guarantee that my depression won't become suicidal and catatonic again. Stabilize me on my medication. Lift my darkness and fear. I turn my life and pain over into your hands. And soon I will be a vessel for you again. I already feel better having approached you. It's been horrible without you. Thank you for all the reminders of you that you sent me today, through Lonnie, and through the nurse who said that nothing is worth killing myself over, and that I'd be hurting my family so bad. God, continue to animate the world around me and I will look for signs of your presence. Thank you for dominoes and card playing today—fellowship that lifted my spirit. Thank you for books and a fine mind, intelligence. Remove my envy and pride. Help me to embrace this baby you put inside me. Help me to accept where I'm at in life. Help me to make better choices today to make tomorrow better. I open my door to you today, God, and I trust that you will banish the dark spirits from my mind and presence. Together we can do this. I love you. I recognize you within and around me. Love, Karla."

Her struggle with her depression continued. It seemed she knew what she had to do, knew how to do it, knew all the right words and thoughts, knew the need for the proper medication, knew the past, present and future of her illness, and knew how to express her feelings clearly. But the struggle remained monumental. We talked with her on the one patients' pay phone as often as they allowed calls, and we could get through the constant busy signal (once or twice a day). She wanted to come home, but we knew that she needed hospitalization until she could get stabilized again. It was painful to talk with her, but we were confident that this present pain would give way to a more balanced, happier Karla. We tried to share this confidence and support with her.

Her journal for January 3, 2003 reflected her struggle:

"Dear God, Ok, I know you already know my pain, but let me tell you anyway that <u>this sucks.</u> I lay in my bed all day, dreading everything. When people ask I just say it sucks. They say depression is anger turned inward. I am so angry apparently. At what? 1. I'm pregnant. 2. I've chopped my hair into this ridiculous burr/buzz cut like I'm a boy or something. 3. I'm gaining weight. 4. I left school. 5. I quit my job. 6. Friendships are poisoned by anger, envy, silence, resentment. 7. I don't have a place of my own. 8. All possible paths look like shit and 9. <u>I am not me.</u> I feel like a statue or a wooden doll. The subconscious mind directs the conscious, and mine is loaded with darkness. Mom and Dad say I have to get stable before I come home—is that even possible? Do I even want to go there? Oh God, what do I do? This is getting old. I feel energies around me, people communicating, and I'm shut out, shut down, hoping no one will talk to me. I don't initiate anything. Mom and Dad's words just roll over me. Lonnie bought me a book today, that guy who wrote the Cosmic Laws Mind book. Why do I have to be bipolar? It really ruins my life.

"I just talked to Mom and Dad. They say: 'Borrow our faith in you. Your hair is not important in the reality of it. You don't have to make any decisions about where you're going to live—let God lead you. Say the serenity prayer.' I admitted that I had been thinking about suicide, and that was why I said I'll go home. Important: I said that if I said better things, I'd feel better.

"10 p.m., time for bed. I'll read my new book.

"Dear God, make it better. I can't, you can, I'm going to let you. Thank you for my parents, even when they get under my skin. Have to go. KS"

In one of our phone calls, she complained about not having enough to do. She wanted something positive that would occupy her mind, something more than reading, and would help her focus on something other than her depression. She suggested studying the bible. That sounded like a good idea to me, but it had to be relatively simple. After talking it over with us, she decided that she would write out the text of the gospel of St. Matthew with very brief summary statements about each section. It wasn't an analysis of the text or even an attempt to apply the message to her life. It was a doable task that helped focus her mind, and she included this project in her journal. From January 4th through January 7th, she summarized chapter 1, verse 1, through chapter 11, verse 27. Her short summary statements do not reflect her depression or struggle; this project was designed to occupy her when she wanted to get away from her demanding and difficult task of dealing with her depression. All indications in her journal and when she talked with us were that this study worked for her. She remained excited about it and commented often that she valued this self-imposed task.

She also continued her journal writing. Her entries from January 5 through 9, many of them in the form of prayers, include these comments:

"I am going to go to school this semester. I want to use my mind. A psych tech said today 'If you don't use it, you lose it!' He's right. All my energies are focused on getting enrolled, getting a part time job, living at Madonna House, and studying the Bible. These are the things I care about. A lot of my problem is boredom. TV and activities that are not directed toward the life I want are not interesting to me. I'm smart and I use my mind. I'll make it. There will be better days than today. Each day gets better. Everyday is better than the last. The medication is working inside me, along with the Bible reading and good pictures of a healthy future. I want peace and joy, and I claim them for myself now. I fall back into the arms of support offered to me by mom, dad, Kevin, Lonnie, Michelle, Swineys … etc. etc … Everywhere I go I make good friends. Having a baby will be a beautiful experience for me … "

" … I knew enough to know that I didn't want to flee from my roots any longer. My roots were, or are, a good place—good values, Catholic Church, education, support—and when I got pregnant I realized that I could lean on my family and on where I come from. Three professional people—and I made up my mind to be one too. I had my sights set on becoming a counselor. The mind follows whatever directions you give it. I started being careful about what I said to myself ... "

"None of us have demons. We have biological, physiological, chemical imbalances. I just learned this while walking ... "

"The staff is doing their best to make sure that suicides and homicides don't happen—it is important work. I respect Dr. Fermo for taking it seriously that I was suicidal recently ... "

" ... I am using this time to build good habits, which is a foundation, like the house built on rocks. Mom and Dad are very supportive. They say just let the pace be slower. They're right. I have patience. I have a structured day and that makes it better. Lonnie can bring me my Latin book. I can be my own counselor. Cindy worked her way through school as a waitress. Discipline. Any place you go is experienced according to your attitude. My attitude is that this treatment is training for my new life ... "

"Just for today I can do things that I would be appalled at if I have to do them for a lifetime. Just for today I can be angry if I want, but it won't help anything if I don't express it, so—I am so PISSED OFF that I cut my hair. There. Now, God, it doesn't really matter, does it? Just for today I will accept my hair cut. Just for today I will stay out of bed. I will read and study the Bible. It's so blessedly quiet right now ... Thank you God that I don't have addictions. The whole ward is next door at a CD (chemically dependent) meeting. (Hey! They just let us smoke!) Keep the mind active. Get out of bed. Go through the motions of getting presentable even though your hair is short. Make the room pleasant. Study the Bible. These are the action steps. Act your way into the right thinking and feeling ... "

"Paddy and Jan came to see me and it was a good visit. I signed over Power of Attorney to my family. They've moved me over to the inpatient unit. I go to court tomorrow. They said my hair looks good! Mom and Dad paid off all my debts! Lonnie loves me! ... "

The following section she titled A Vision of my Life, and it was written on January 7, 2003:

"I wake up and go for a walk (or maybe I walk later in the day). I go to work where I work with people who need my help. I take classes a couple days a week. I see a friend for dinner. I run some errands. I end the day reading for school, relaxing. I go to an Al-Anon meeting. I study yoga. I take dance classes. I make some phone calls to people who live out of town. I go to church. I laugh a lot. I speak with confidence. I have friends. I enjoy my job. I have plans for the next step. I call my parents. I talk to Kevin. I pray. I study the Bible. I get right out of bed in the morning, take a shower, get ready for the day. At night I fall into bed exhausted, but it's a good feeling. On weekends I see a play or a movie, or I take a road trip. I pay for my own life. I manage my finances. I'm serene, courageous, and wise. I'm a survivor. I'm a child of God."

On January 8, she wrote:

" ... I won't be in and out of these places all my life because: 1) I will take my meds 2) I have a strong support system 3) I am smart 4) I am educated 5) God won't be outdone in generosity. First the actions: I'll take my Latin final; I'll finish my essay. I'll enroll, even if late. I'll take classes, get my degree. I'll get a desk job, something inside and comfortable. I'll give my baby a home like I can't provide. It will all come. It will turn around. I've learned what I don't want ... "

And then on January 9, in another "Dear God" entry, she prayed:

"We are all a depressive episode away from the Salvation Army and the Day Shelter for the Homeless. Today's been a hard day—I hate getting up in the morning. Bed is not available. Depressed today. Why? Laid in bed and thought about Art, OSU, my house, IHOP—my classes, good grades, being beautiful, having friends—and now I don't have any of that.

"Oh God, turn me around again. Colin said that looking back is not good. This book I'm reading is good. What do I have going on today? What shall I tell the doctor? Colin says I'll get out of this. I have a hard time picturing my life. Structure, good habits, Millicent said today. Have to get a job, get my degree. Can I do all this without beauty? I wish I could be beautiful again. How do I face the world looking ordinary? Look how screwed up my priorities are. I just saw the doctor. I'm getting out tomorrow. Love, Karla."

The last two sentences of this entry continue to haunt me. They are totally inconsistent with everything that precedes these final words.

The last entry in her journal was the evening of Friday, January 10, after she returned to Madonna House:

"My God, my God I am home. Not by external circumstances may I judge your kingdom or my place in it, but by the graces you bestow, my closeness to you, Holy Father.

"I am so blessed by your gifts I receive every day. You have wrestled me free from the hands of death and placed me in the loving care of beautiful people. All around me I feel the blessedness of your gifts to me.

"Make my soul clean as I sleep, restful dreams and thoughts await me. Your infinite kindness brushes my cheek so I rest. The angels stand by to praise you with me.

"I am home, loved by many, and healing. Thank God. Thank you, Jesus, for another day. Amen. Love, Karla."

There are no entries for the weekend of January 11 and 12.

Her January journal reflects her inner life during the first ten days of 2003. While she was recording her battle with depression, Fran, Kevin, and I were also talking with the staff of the Tulsa Center for Behavioral Health. We had been dealing with Karla's illness for seven years, and through many frightening episodes, we learned the way she thought, how she presented herself, and what she needed to regain health. We are not doctors or psychiatrists, of course, but we were very familiar with how Karla experienced her bipolar life. All three of us tried to share that unique knowledge with the doctors, nurses, and staff of TCBH.

For example, a few days after she was accepted into the hospital, Karla indicated that she wanted to be released into our care and move to Belleville. While it was very attractive that she would be with us, and we could get her appropriate care here, we knew she needed to stay in the hospital there. We talked with a number of people on staff at TCBH, particularly Dr. Fermo, and they agreed that an early release would be dangerous. A few days later, Karla admitted that had she been released, she was planning to kill herself.

When she was transferred to the inpatient section of the Center, we were pleased because that transfer implied to us that she would remain under supervised, inpatient care for some time, at least another week or so. We were relieved.

A Shocking Release from Treatment

We were also mistaken. They released her two days later, on Friday, January 10 and notified us after the decision was made. We strenuously objected. She needed more time for the medications to take hold, and she needed a more structured environment for a little longer. And there was no monitored plan for the weekend. She was scheduled to begin aftercare on January 13 at 3:00 p.m..

She, of course, was thrilled to leave. To her, it was a sign that she was starting the next phase of her life. To us, it was a danger sign. We were aware that suicide was more likely when victims were getting a little stronger, as opposed to when they were in the depth of depression. That was precisely the position Karla was in that weekend. We were very nervous about her release and talked to her often during those days.

There was sadness in her voice during those calls, but she sounded like she was doing okay. The Madonna House staff was very helpful, and she planned to register for school on Monday morning. She said that she had some nausea and vomited a little on Sunday morning. We figured she was experiencing some morning sickness due to her pregnancy. Our friend Margie, pointed out during the day on Sunday that Karla was probably losing some of her medication through the morning sickness. Fran and I called Karla around ten o'clock Sunday night to alert her to that possibility and urged her to call her doctor at TCBH for advice. I don't know if she made that call.

Monday, January 13, 2003

We're still not sure what happened Monday morning but she did her chores at Madonna House faithfully and left around 8:00 a.m. to register for class. Some hours later she arrived at Lonnie's apartment, and they talked. She apparently felt unable to commit to the classes she had to take and didn't go to school. They talked about it for quite awhile, and he assured her that she didn't have to go to school at this time. Lonnie didn't think she was overly depressed or despondent. He had to leave to do some work at his father's farm and planned to come back in time to take her to her first aftercare session at 3:00 p.m..

On January 13, 2003, a dreary, damp, overcast Monday, with the temperature at 40 degrees, around 1:00 p.m., in a faded blue, windowless, bare, cinder block bedroom just large enough for a king-size bed, a bedroom converted from a store room in a vending machine repair shop and warehouse, in an aging industrial section of the west end of Tulsa, Oklahoma, our twenty-six-year-old, beautiful, charming, loving, occasionally brilliant, multi-talented, bipolar daughter found a hidden, .22 caliber rifle, propped it up between the bed spring and the mattress, rested it on her chest, reached down, pulled the trigger probably with her right thumb and died instantly as the bullet ripped through her body, severing her aorta with what the medical examiner later described as a "perforating contact gunshot wound of the chest".

A little after 5:00 that evening, I got home from the office. Ten minutes later, a policeman rang the doorbell. I thought Fran had been in an accident. He told me that he had no details but that "Karla Smith had passed away." I yelled something unintelligible, could not remain standing, and fell on the couch, repeating that she must have killed herself and sobbing convulsively. The officer tried to console me, but it wasn't possible.

A few minutes later Fran came home, and I told her that Karla had died. Her reaction was similar to mine: tears and shock. It dawns on me now: we both believed the report. We did not accept her death emotionally (I still haven't accepted it completely), but we knew the report was true. Karla was dead.

10

That Week

While Fran and I tried to grasp the immediate impact of the news of Karla's suicide, the officer called Fr. Bill Hitpas, our pastor and a friend of mine since high school, who arrived at the house within twenty minutes. I had to call Margie because we were scheduled to conduct a meeting of the Pastoral Council at St. Agatha's parish in New Athens, one of the parishes in the Belleville diocese. She cancelled the meeting and came to our house. Fran called my sister Sharon, and her friend Janie, and they came right over. The officer left and it was Fr. Bill, Margie, Sharon, Janie, Fran, and I. I was grateful for all of them even though their presence was not actually consoling. Her death was too new and too raw for me to be consoled. But I was glad they were there; their presence helped me absorb some of the shock. Group grieving is sometimes more valuable than personal grieving, even when it feels more like shock than grief.

Telling Kevin

We had to tell Kevin. He was on a project in Milwaukee, a fortunate assignment as it turned out, because Fran is from Milwaukee and has three sisters and a brother there, along with multiple in-laws, nephews, and nieces. We called Kevin and got his voice mail. I tried to leave a message that insisted he call home quickly, but I certainly didn't want to tell him what happened through a recorded message.

We called Julie, Fran's sister, who went to Miller Brewery where Kevin was working in order to be with him that night after we talked to him. He called back shortly. He said later that he knew when he heard my message. We had been very worried about Karla after they released her.

The only way I can describe his reaction, and then my reaction to him, is that we wailed together. Long, loud, haunting, guttural sounds, emanating from the soul, traveling slowly through the abdomen, chest, lungs, throat, head, nose, gaining momentum and strength, picking up a shape, a resonance, a nuance, a depth as it journeyed through every speck of the body and finally erupting from the mouth, unformed, indiscriminate, toneless because it incorporated all tones and echoed the inconsolable cry of all grief-stricken people of all times. We wailed. It was primal, prehistoric, and futuristic. It still reverberates in my being. For a long time, we wailed.

The rest of that night was spent being numb. Fran called her family. Kevin, we learned, spent the night with Julie, Pat and Jack, his aunts and uncle. I wanted more details—how, when, where, who was there, and infiltrating every other question, why did she do it? There was no continuing discussion about any of these questions, just periodic references to parts of them. We prayed together for Karla, for us, and for some measure of consolation. We are all believers in a loving God, even in the middle of a tragedy like this. The shock, pain, loss, anger and regret do not minimize my faith in a God who loves, forgives, and understands. I believed that the night of January 13, 2003, and I still believe it today. Strangely, that faith is only somewhat consoling. Karla's death remains a permanent hole in my world, a chasm that even God can not bridge. It is now an unalterable reality, just like the reality that I am a 5'10" tall, male Caucasian with brown eyes. Karla Smith remains dead, even though I believe she lives eternally with God. The Karla I know is gone. My acceptance of this new reality is far from complete. Belief in God does not remove that pain.

Suicide

Ultimately, she shot herself because she suffered from bipolar illness. Many illnesses kill people—cancer, diabetes, heart disease all take their grizzly toll on millions of victims who leave more millions of people grieving. The causal connection between these diseases and death is obvious. If someone dies of cancer, there is immediate understanding that this loss has a clear reason. With mental illness, that connection is not usually assumed. According to the World Health Organization (2002) *World Report on Violence and Health* "suicide worldwide causes more deaths every year than homicide or war." Even that staggering comparison does not eliminate the suspicion that suicide is not the drastic end of an illness but a freely chosen act of a guilty self-murderer. The implication is that the diseased person goes to her grave tarnished, deserving some punishment because she is not really a victim but a criminal.

Even for people who do not accept this rigid judgment of a "suicider" there often remains some suspicion. I heard it between the lines of some of the sympathy messages people shared during Karla's wake and in some of the notes people sent us. People didn't mean any harm and they certainly were not blunt or overtly condemnatory. But occasionally I heard it. A suicide raises questions that a heart attack doesn't. "Karla was responsible for her death," they think. I become the father of a beautiful young woman who unfairly forced this grief on me, and therefore they sympathize with me. Most of the time this accusation is subtle and unintended, but it is there. If she had died of cystic fibrosis, there would be no such suspicion.

The stigma attached to Karla's suicide reflects a well-documented attitude in our society. The President's New Freedom Commission on Mental Health in its final report *Achieving the Promise: Transforming Mental Health Care in America (July 2003)* is so concerned about this attitude that they identify changing our view of mental illness as their first recommendation. "Stigma refers to a cluster of negative attitudes and beliefs that motivate the general public to fear, reject, avoid, and discriminate against people with mental illnesses. Stigma is widespread in the United States and other Western nations." (United States Public Health Service Office of the Surgeon General (2001), *Mental Health: Culture, Race, and Ethnicity: A Supplement to Mental Health: A Report of the Surgeon General.* Rockville, MD: Department of Health and Human Services: U.S. Public Health Service.)

I don't claim to know Karla's mind. For seven years I struggled to understand, and I know I made some progress. She wanted us to understand, to see the world and herself as she did. She was a passionate communicator. I tried but it was and remains difficult. I am convinced that she is not guilty. She died of bipolar illness. Her death by bipolar was not inevitable; she could have and should have survived this depressive episode. She would have been a productive citizen, devoted wife, loving mother, and successful author. And, in my opinion, she died innocent.

One of the questions that swirled around my disjointed spirit that first night revolved around a possible suicide note. Since she was a prolific writer, surely she wanted to document her last act. So I thought. But there was no note, although she deleted some files from her computer that morning. (Later we retrieved these files and there still was no note. There were some articles, notes, ideas that she no longer wanted—more of an editing process than a suicide letter.)

She probably didn't write a note that morning because she wrote the one on December 31 when Fran first admitted her to the hospital. She wanted to shoot herself then but couldn't do it. My guess is that after only nine days in the hospital and beginning some new meds, she felt basically the same as she did on New Year's Eve, but she was now strong enough to act more stable and fool the staff of the hospital. Her New Year's Eve suicide note was still operative on January 13. Even though we talked with her daily on the phone, including the night before she died, and even though she sounded a little better, the despair recorded in her suicide letter still haunted her on January 13. The result of that despair is tragically obvious.

Funeral Planning

As the week of her death unfolded, the combination of grief, funeral preparations, visitors, and phone calls crashed in on us like ten-foot waves pounding the jagged boulders of a rugged, Pacific coastline. Fran, Kevin, and I are action-oriented people; we get things done, usually with some competence and efficiency. These skills were valuable as we made plans for her wake and funeral even as we tried to make some initial adjustments to a life without Karla. I cried regularly—sometimes almost predictably and other times when I least expected it. Over the decades I have worked hard at trying to identify and express my feelings, but during that week, I could only identify numbness interrupted by volcanoes of unannounced and unnamed sadness.

Fran's brothers, sisters, and in-laws arrived from all over the country. Pat and Jack drove down from Milwaukee while Betty flew in from Knoxville, Tennessee. Tom and Kathy caught a flight out of Seattle and Mary and her husband, Tom also drove from Milwaukee. Fran's brother Jim with his wife, Ro joined us from Chicago. Her sister Julie made driving arrangements with Kelly and Peggy, two of her daughters and Peggy's friend Eric. Fr. Bob Hart, her brother and a Jesuit priest, was unable to come because of health complications due to his Parkinson's disease.

The Hart family combined with my sister Sharon, and her friend Janie, and my other sister Rosie, to comfort us but also to deal with their own loss of Karla. Karla relished being part of these two families, including the Smiths, Grimms, and Lodes' from my side, and even though her behavior was erratic at various points, the families loved and accepted her. Many of these people were in our living room on Friday night after the wake, and their presence, stories, songs, condolences, and practical help made that week, and especially that night, livable—and, for brief moments, enjoyable. I always valued those relationships; after that week I treasure them.

Ginny Cusack, a dear friend of Fran's for over thirty years, immediately flew in from Princeton, New Jersey, and gave us her complete, service-oriented attention and support for a whole week. My co-workers, Kelly, Patti, Sue, JoAnn, and Greg, brought food to the house, provided and managed the food and beverage during the wake, and covered my responsibilities at the office for the week or so when I couldn't even think about the diocesan planning project, RENEW, the Diocesan Pastoral Council, Parish Pastoral Council workshops, or the budget. They also, and most sensitively, kept me supplied with raspberry tea.

Literally hundreds of other people interacted with us during that week. Some of Kevin's friends mingled in and out of our family, and they kept us grounded and supported. Over five hundred cards and letters arrived, many of them containing donations to the Bipolar Alliance (to help fight the illness which haunted Karla), Our Lady Queen of Peace Endowment Fund (the school for which Fran was principal and in order to promote education which was so important to Karla) or Catholic Urban Programs (in recognition of her commitment to the poor). Our 332 thank-you notes weeks later did not begin to express our gratitude.

We wanted to help design the wake service and funeral liturgy. Since Fran and I worked for the Catholic Church in a variety of ways for most of our lives, we knew something about liturgy, and we had some ideas about the funeral. Fr. Bill was extremely helpful and empathetic throughout the whole process (even when the phone kept interrupting our planning). He was then and continues to be today a remarkable example of a truly gifted pastor—intelligent, thoughtful, compassionate, faith-filled, and articulate. At a time when Catholic priests have lost some public respect, Bill remains the good shepherd.

Kevin's Wake Service Eulogy

From the very beginning of this ordeal, Kevin said he wanted to do the eulogy for his twin sister. I had spoken at the funerals of my mom, dad, and sister but I was glad to relinquish this bitter (not sweet!) responsibility to him. His tribute to Karla at the wake service was simply outstanding. He combined his love for her with a description of who she was and wasn't, and included a gripping portrayal of her illness. Here is his complete text:

"**Life** is what happens to you when you have other plans. None of us in this room tonight planned to be here when we began our week on Monday. And yet, what happened to us this week is that **life** got in the way of our plans. Now to some of you, this analogy of **life** may seem confusing at such a tragic time. We are here at a place of death. But to my dear twin sister, Karla, it would be as clear as her crystal blue eyes. You see, Karla had that ability to look beyond what seemed so obvious to all of us. She had that power to see the world from a different perspective. And she had the wisdom to interpret what it all meant. And then with all of her excitement and passion, she would explain it to you. And she would explain it again. And again. Until you understood. Until she knew that you saw the meaning. And she'd walk away and you'd sit there for a minute … and then you'd smile … and you'd think, 'Wow, I never really thought of it like that before.' And so tonight, as we see death and we feel pain, I invite you to come with me and see the deeper meaning of **life** that Karla would have seen. And even though she'd probably explain it better than me, I think I've learned enough from her throughout the years that she will help me through it.

"Before we journey back into the **life** of Karla, I'd like to tell you a little bit about why we are gathered here tonight. Bipolar disorder, also known as manic-depressive illness, brings suffering to nearly two million Americans. Studies indicate that another one million minds are also haunted, but not yet detected. Its symptoms include irregular mood swings ranging from high periods of manic intensity to deep, overwhelming depression. Medically speaking, and I'm not a medical speaker, the brain does not produce the right chemicals to allow you to process thoughts at rational levels. The cause for this is unknown. Though medications can help offset the illness, nearly all bipolar individuals struggle to continually take their medicine on a regular basis.

Any break in the daily pattern can quickly lead to extreme, unstable thoughts and actions. There is no cure for bipolar disorder.

"During one of Karla's recent manic episodes this past August, she stayed at my house in St. Louis for two nights. As she frantically moved from story to story, task to task, and explanation to explanation without sleeping in between, I calmed her down enough and asked her, 'Karla, tell me how you feel right now. Describe your mind to me.' She said, 'Kev, I just can't explain it. It's so exciting and invigorating and intense. I hear everything clearer, I see everything better, I know everything deeper, I react faster' … and then after a brief pause, she said, 'and even though I want it to stop, I just can't stop it.' I asked, 'Karla, how can I help you break this?' And she gave me a perplexed look and said,

"'OK, Kev, it's like this … imagine your mind as a switchboard and you are looking right at it. And on this switchboard is everything that has ever happened in your **life**—every past thought, every past event, every past emotion. And one flash appears on the switchboard so you focus on it, but 10 seconds later, another flash appears, and you have to look at it, but then there's another flash over there, and another one here, and another—and your mind pushes you to see all of them because you have to see them all and experience them all. It's constant. And I try to explain my thoughts, and what is going on, but it's so hard to speak that fast because my **life** is too confusing.'

"I listened in disbelief and wondered how I could possibly imagine. But at least now I understood. Karla always made it easy for me to understand. She was so good like that.

"Bipolar disorder is mental torture. The demons and voices and anguish don't disappear. Karla spoke of these often. In a letter she wrote to me in 1997 in the midst of another bipolar battle, she began:

"'It's hard for me to talk out loud. There's a rock that lives in my throat. My mind races with illogical half sentences, and I cannot keep up with it. I am afraid of everything, have panic freak-outs about things I used to do with ease, and I'm afraid of even people that I'm closest to. I often don't answer the phone or call anyone back. I'm not afraid of one specific thing, but instead a big general fear—that's how it's been inside.'

"So far I've described more of the manic side of bipolar disorder, the extreme opposite depression side needs no further explanation. Tragically, 1 out of every 5 bipolar individuals takes his/her own life. So if we think about that statistic through Karla's eyes, I guess she decided she would give **life** to four other bipolar individuals instead. That's just the way she was. She was so good like that.

"The Karla to remember, however, was not one inflicted with bipolar disorder. And even though we would see glimpses of the true Karla during her bipolar episodes, the high majority of her physical being on earth was truly poetry in motion. But before I tell you about all that Karla WAS in her **life**, I first want to tell you a few of the things that she WAS NOT …

"Karla WAS NOT the older twin. Born Aug. 7, 1976, at 7:40 a.m., and even though Mom asked the doctor for a day of rest in between, Karla was 10 minutes younger than me and 8 ounces lighter. I used to joke and tell her it was the best 10 minutes of my **life** and even though she smiled every time … we both knew it was 10 minutes in which something was missing.

"Karla WAS NOT the quiet type as a child. Big shocker, I know. She was always the adventurer, even in her younger days. Exploring, questioning, creating, acting, dancing were among her favorites as she searched and found new activities, friends, and places almost every day. As high school transitioned into her college, Karla grew into the individual that so clearly defined her beautiful character. As she neared the completion of her English degree from Oklahoma St. University, one thing she certainly WAS NOT was a business woman. Numerous were the times when we would debate her disdain for capitalism, her dislike for 9–5 jobs, and her questioning about what really was the purpose of business. 'What was the benefit of any of that stuff?', she would say. 'Why does **life** even have to include money? Why can't we all just share everything and be happy?' Well, Karla, it's another good idea and one that we should probably all think about a little bit more. She made it so easy and simple to understand. It was that simplicity that made her **life** so rich. She was so good like that.

"Another thing that Karla definitely WAS NOT was a sports fan. Oh boy, did I try. For twenty-six years I tried. When I'd convince her to play ping-pong with me—of course, we couldn't keep score and the game would last at the most five minutes. When I tried to get her to shoot baskets—she'd do cartwheels. When I'd try to explain to her how awesome one of my weekend sports event excursions had been, she'd jokingly ask, 'What sport was that?'. And after five straight years, I just stopped trying to explain fantasy football to her. But through it all, she knew. And I knew. And that's what made our twinness so unique. Though I am a lot of the things in **life** that she WAS NOT, we accepted it in each other, we learned from it, we laughed about it, and we let it make us closer. We just had that balance. We were so good like that.

"As Karla often reminded me, a good writer has the knowledge to understand everything about a situation and be able to convince her audience what is most important. Karla WAS so many things. I believe that the true essence of a person is not measured by tangible possessions or accomplishments; rather a person is measured by their intangible qualities. Karla WAS beauty in every sense of the word, even when everyone else around her could see it and she couldn't. She just had this way about her, this sparkle of **life** in her eye, which even people who had barely known her could see. If we could have only kept a count of the multitudes of people to whom Karla gave that sparkle, we'd fill an ocean. But then, it wouldn't be Karla. You see, Karla much preferred the anonymous connection she had with people. It was the eighty-year-old man at the Irish pub, or the pregnant teenager working at Arby's, or the Bosnian women who couldn't speak English, or the homeless man who needed a sandwich, or the physically handicapped college student who needed help getting to class—these were Karla's people. These were the people to whom she opened her arms, shared the little money she had, and gave them hope. She did it because she understood people and she understood **life**. And she cared, she just cared. She was so good like that. So good.

"Another thing Karla WAS was coffee. Oh man, could she drink that stuff. At any time and any place and with anyone. Honestly, I don't really think she even liked the taste that much—but what it signified to her was **LIFE**. It was her avenue to debate, philosophize, relax, theorize, write, connect, analyze, and study. A cup of coffee with Karla was your chance to be enlightened. To be enriched. To see from a profound perspective. To understand the world the way it was meant to be understood. To hear it like it was. Karla touched so many people with her coffee—and it's that coffee that I want you to remember and take with you—because that was **life**.

"Karla WAS a seeker. She sought the knowledge in books—literature, poetry, stories, history. She yearned for it and became who she was through it. She found harmony in music, especially through favorite female artists such as Ani Defranco, Tori Amos, Indigo Girls, and Sarah McLaughlin. A stereo was never too far away and phrases such as, 'you gotta come listen to the words of this song' were often said excitedly. And through all of her seeking in music and books, there was one common thread which tied it all together—her quest for spirituality. This search took many different forms throughout her journey, and those of you who shared her coffee understand what I mean. During the last couple of months, she told me that she had taken comfort in reading the Bible, specifically the New Testament. She said that she had rededicated her **life** and wanted to be confirmed again as a Catholic. I like to think that perhaps this was her way of telling me that she had finally found what she had been searching for all these years.

"See, what Karla did is she took all of these intangible qualities and she aspired to write. To document her ideas and explain it so the rest of the world could understand. It was her passion and she was so good at it. Though her writings were never published and many are scattered, as part of our Tribute to Karla tonight I wanted you all to have a small sampling of how she spent so many of her precious hours—only because I know it's what she would want. Please take a copy of 'Karla's Memoirs' as you leave tonight. The five poems written by Karla were selected not as a way to intensify our pain, but rather as a way for Karla to inspire your own **life**. She was so good like that.

"And as we celebrate Karla's **life** during the next two days, we still have the same burning question in our minds. Why? Why Karla? Why now? It certainly is a question I wish I didn't have to answer, yet maybe as a result of the past few minutes we are beginning to look at this day the way that Karla would. Maybe we just needed to look a little bit deeper than our initial thoughts. Maybe Karla knew that the torments of a long **life** battling an incurable disorder would never really allow her to spread the love she wanted to spread. Maybe she out-thought us again. Maybe her last selfless act was to give us all a reason to come together, to look at our own lives, to encourage us to bury our own demons. To maybe encourage each one of us to live a bit more humbly, to take more **life** adventures, to take the trip we are debating on taking, and to mend a broken relationship. Maybe it was because she wanted Mom, Dad, and me to feel the overwhelming sense of love and support we have felt from all of you this week. Not maybe, I know it was—because it's something she would have thought about. Karla knew me better than anyone in this world, and I will miss her physical presence more than anything I've ever missed. Yet, I think she gave me enough **life** over the past twenty-six years to last forever—and I hope I'm not the only one who feels that way.

"Karla always believed in symbolism. In some of her recent writings, her main message to me has been to 'Be Strong'. It's taken strength to write this, a lot of strength that I believe was inspired by her. I want everyone to know that in my tribute to her tonight, I haven't forgotten about her precious symbolism. I know Karla would tell me that you aren't supposed to explain the symbolism to your audience, but in this case I have to break the rule. The acute listeners and readers will have noticed my repeated mentioning of one particular, important word—**life**. The first word of my tribute was **life** and so too will it be the last word—because that is why we are here to celebrate. And in total you'll hear twenty-six times when I use the word, which represent each of Karla's twenty-six wonderful years. I know Karla wouldn't have needed this explanation, she would have figured it out right away—because she was so good like that.

"I'm going to close with a story, a dream actually. I've never been one to remember my dreams when I sleep. It's very rare. But on the night I heard of Karla's passing, in the brief amount of time that I actually slept, I did have a dream I'll always remember. I was driving Karla to the airport and she was in a frantic state of mind because she was running late and didn't want to miss her flight. I woke up several times, but each time went back to sleep and continued the same dream. I was so determined to get her there because I knew she depended on me. We made it just in time, and I watched her board her plane and take-off. When I awoke, the symbolism struck me. I've always had this image of God as a man in a long, white robe floating up in the heavens with His arms open. I want you to picture Karla flying towards him, stepping off her one-way flight, falling into His arms, crying softly for a minute, looking up at Him, and finally, finally knowing that she will be at peace for the rest of her **life**."

Hundreds and hundreds of people attended the wake and funeral—Karla's friends, Kevin's friends, classmates from high school and college, co-workers, our relatives and friends and co-workers. They came from Massachusetts, Texas, Oklahoma, Kansas, Iowa, Wisconsin, New Jersey, North Carolina, Missouri, and of course, Illinois. They listened with uncommon attention as Kevin courageously shared his feelings about his sister as well as his personal knowledge of her illness. As his father, I listened with pride and sorrow as the body of his twin lay in her coffin a few feet behind his podium. The impact on his audience was universal. There was support and admiration throughout the room, into the hallways and overflowing into a neighboring parlor. He said what he had to say, and he said it extremely well.

www. inmemoryofkarlasmith.com

Within a week of the funeral, Kevin and his friend Jay, did something that I didn't even think was possible. They created a Web site dedicated to the memory of Karla. It includes some recent pictures (including a shot of Kevin and Karla at Paradise Point), his wake service tribute to her, his farewell letter which he delivered during the funeral mass the next day, the prayers Fran and I wrote and shared during her funeral, a short booklet containing five of her poems, and links to bipolar sites. Another feature continues to offer us daily consolation—they included a simple procedure for people to "light a candle" in her memory. Viewing those candles with the names and messages of the people who "lit" them is a modern marvel melding the supposedly impersonal world of computers with the warmth and affection of compassionate people.

I urge you to visit the site, look at the pictures, read the documents, and light a candle. The address is: inmemoryofkarlasmith.com. When you do it, you will see what I mean.

The Funeral Liturgy

The funeral liturgy was all we asked for and more. Fr. Bill was the celebrant and set a tone of solemnity and hope. His homily was spectacular, reminding us that God knows and accepts our pain so that we don't move too quickly and disastrously into a pseudo-consolation of faith and resurrection. God is with us as we struggle. Hope is real but it springs from the pain that is also real. Many priest friends participated in the funeral liturgy, and Bishop Wilton Gregory also spoke with genuine compassion and eloquence.

Fran and I composed and led the prayers of intercession. We wanted to capture some of her most striking qualities and turn them into prayers for all of us. Here's what we prayed:

"1) Remembering Karla's love of knowledge and her persistent search for truth, we ask that we too may always seek truth, we pray to the Lord …

2) Remembering Karla's quiet but active compassion for the poor, we ask that, as individuals and as communities, we act more compassionately to all people, especially those who live on the fringe of society, we pray to the Lord …

3) Remembering Karla's commitment to the value of relationships, we look to our own relationships in the hope that we may care for each other better, accept each other more, and forgive each other sooner, we pray to the Lord …

4) Remembering Karla's deep-seated and life-long search for spiritual wholeness, we renew our search for traces of God within ourselves, within the experiences of our lives and within the events of our world, we pray to the Lord …

5) Remembering Karla's heartfelt passion for justice, we strive to open our hearts and take action for people who are marginalized, rejected, victimized or simply ignored, we pray to the Lord …

6) Remembering Karla's ability to live simply, without the desire for luxury, we examine our own desires in order to identify and remove unwarranted longings for things and possessions, we pray to the Lord … "

We had a hard time getting through these prayers, but we made it. The crowded church prayed with us with sincerity and sadness.

Toward the end of the funeral service, Kevin added one more personal message—a farewell letter to his sister:

"Dear Karla,

"Oh, how you would have enjoyed the service we had in your honor last night. There was so much love. It extended out the door, into the hallway, and even into another room. My—how you touched lives in this world. People have come from all over the United States just to pay you tribute. It is truly amazing. This world can be so good sometimes. We even handed out some of your poetry (200 copies to be exact), so consider yourself published now. And the love has continued even this morning with many more gathered here in the House of God. But you know what you would have liked the best? The true sincerity, support, kindness, generosity, and hope that so many people have given to Mom, Dad, and me over the past week. It has been overwhelming. And yet even in this tragic time, I think that just coming together has helped not only our family, but so many others who also mourn your loss. The exit of your physical life will help other people live a better physical life, and I know that will make you proud.

"In my tribute speech to you last night, I told everyone about your belief in symbolism. It certainly wasn't easy meeting with the funeral directors earlier this week, but we tried to keep your symbolism in mind as we made our decisions. For your prayer cards we chose the prayer you prayed daily, The Serenity Prayer, and we even added your own personal version to your 'Memoirs' booklet we distributed last night. Personally, I kinda like your version better. The flowers from Mom, Dad, and me included 'Birds of Paradise' which represented your free-spirit and love of animals. The casket selection—well, that was daunting, but as soon as we saw the different casket names—that decision was actually the easiest. Yours is called 'Simplicity', for through your simplicity, you've given us all a unique richness. And of course it's made of wood. Your final resting place will be close to other family members at Lakeview Memorial Gardens in a special section called the "Garden of Peace"—we know it's what you wanted.

"There's one last piece of symbolism we'd like to give you, but it will require the help of everyone gathered in the church today. We know how much your world was a stage, so we thought it might be nice to give you one final curtain call before we go. So this is what we'll do. As I call the group which represents you, please stand and remain standing, but hold your applause as I will explain that later:

"All of your aunts and uncles, please stand ...

All of your cousins, please stand ...

All of your friends from Stillwater and Oklahoma City please stand ...

All of your friends from Bishop Kelley, please stand ...

All of your friends who knew you from the Tulsa area, please
stand ...
All people from your birth city of Ottumwa, Iowa, please stand ...
All of your brother's friends and co-workers, please stand ...
All co-workers of your mom and dad, please stand ...
All friends of your mom and dad, please stand ...
All St. Nicholas parishioners, please stand ...
All of other supporters of you and our Smith family, please stand ...

"That should leave all but two, and they say that in theatre they
save the best for last—so finally, would your parents please stand.
Through this all, you have stood tall because this type of thing is not
supposed to happen to a parent. Family is the backbone of our world.
And we will get through this as we've done thus far—by doing it
together.

"So, Karla, you should see it now. The whole church is standing
for you. This time, however, their applause will sound different as we
ask them all to join hands and applaud in song—your favorite church
hymn, 'Amazing Grace.'

Your loving brother always,
Kevin"

Sitting in the first pew with Karla's coffin a few feet away was
extremely difficult. When Kevin ended his farewell letter to her, the
three of us gathered around the coffin, placed our hands on her
wooden tomb while the congregation sang "Amazing Grace." I could
not sing very well. I remembered the verse to a song Karla and I composed years earlier, when she was eight or nine. She went with me on
a business trip to a parish in Antlers, OK, where I conducted a work-
shop on Pastoral Councils. During the long four-hour drive there and
back we sang songs and made up our own verse to "When I First
Came to the Land ... " Our verse was about my daughter who was
"sparkling water." As the congregation sang a poignant version of

"Amazing Grace," my heart hummed a different tune about a daughter and some sparkling water.

It was snowing when we left St. Nicholas church and led a long procession to Lakeview Memorial Gardens. We gathered in the chapel rather than at the gravesite for our final prayers and thanks to all who attended the funeral that Saturday morning.

Of all the details surrounding her funeral, I want to mention just one more. Karla was an off-and-on participant in Al-Anon. She moved so often that she got away from her home group in Broken Arrow, OK, but she knew the program, read the literature, and tried to practice the twelve steps. She prayed the Serenity Prayer often, and being both unique and a writer, she composed her own prayer by adding to the traditional petitions. Her version prays like this:

God grant me the serenity to accept the things I cannot change,
Courage to change the things I can,
And wisdom to know the difference.

Show me the trace of you in everyone I know.
Gently turn my gaze back home,
Toward simplicity, grace, and gratitude.
Remind me that we are all imperfect, holy, and free.
Open me to know and embrace your peace.

When we had to choose the epitaph for the marker on her grave, we quickly thought of this prayer. If you ever visit her gravesite at Lakeview Memorial Gardens in Fairview Heights, IL, go to the section called Peace, and you will find her grave just below the graves of my parents and my brother Roy. And on the marker you will read: Gently turn my gaze back home, toward simplicity, grace, and gratitude. She is now home where simplicity, grace, and gratitude are the normal course of existence.

A Sad Trip to Tulsa

That tragic weekend ended with friends and relatives returning home. We had to go to Tulsa to take care of her stuff, sell her car, and retrieve the material the police took when they investigated her death. Ginny, thank heavens, went with us. We borrowed Kevin's 4Runner and drove the four hundred miles to Tulsa, picked up some of her clothes, notions, and a few mementoes from Madonna House, and checked into a motel some Tulsa friends provided for us. It was 9:00 p.m., Ginny and I were hungry (Fran preferred taking a relaxing bath), and we walked to a restaurant next to the motel. I had some chili. Some bad chili. I was sick all night and through most of the next day. Fran and Ginny sold Karla's 1990 Honda Accord to a generous used car dealer whom Fran knew from her years as principal of All Saints school in Broken Arrow. They also went to the Property Room of the Tulsa County police station where they picked up a large plastic box that contained the material the police confiscated when they investigated Karla's death.

When they returned to the motel room in the early afternoon, I was feeling a little better physically but disappointed that I wasn't able to help with these distressing chores. I was grateful they accomplished all they did, especially selling the car which I thought was going to be a problem.

But the most difficult stop was yet to come, and there was no way I was going to miss it. We had to go to the place where she died, Lonnie's apartment/warehouse. He told me later that he took his .22 rifle to his dad's farm, like he promised me on New Year's Eve. But a few days before Karla shot herself, someone broke into the warehouse and Lonnie felt he needed to retrieve the gun for his own protection. He hid it where he thought she couldn't find it, but obviously he was wrong. He discovered her body, went into shock but immediately called the police. He was quickly cleared of any negligence or involvement in her suicide.

Lonnie was there when we arrived the afternoon of January 21. Standing in the small, bare, cinder block bedroom where she died, I slowly sank into a swirling awareness that this was where she took her last breath. I was there, in the hospital room in Ottumwa, Iowa, when she took her first breath. That beautiful 4 pound 13 oz miracle stopped breathing in this cramped, dreary bedroom 26 years later. I sobbed. I didn't recall any specifics of those 26 years; I didn't even have a clear picture of her in my mind. My memory was simply not working. I felt suspended but surrounded by absence. The hole in my soul expanded until the absence swallowed my body, mind, feelings and spirit. It was Paradise Point reversed. It was tapestry unraveled. I still don't know how long this state of intense pain lasted. At some point, I moved on to the sad tasks at hand, but actually, that feeling of abandonment never ended. Periodically, it reappears even now.

We loaded the SUV, returned to the motel and headed for Interstate 44 and home the next morning. Ginny drove and for the next five hours, I read a manuscript we found that Karla had written. It was a first draft, and I know she was going to edit and change her approach in the final version. We had talked about it a few times a year earlier. The working title was "To Whom It May Concern, A Personal Letter to the Chosen Suffering from Depression." As I read it out loud, the three of us relished the written contact with the deceased author. In chapter 5, What Are You?, she wrote:

"Your relationship with yourself has been damaged so severely that, in a sense, you need to start over. Again, what you think of yourself is not true. The part of yourself to consult first to know the truth about you is that still, small voice at the core of who you are. It cannot lead you astray. Perhaps you have not heard it in years, but I would suggest that you have, and you have only let other voices sound louder within you. You turn up the volume of the Should Voice, the Should Have Voice, as well as the I Need, the I Am Less Than, and the I Can't Voices. Underneath all that needless static, the true, still, small voice is straining to be heard.

"It is the voice that God implanted within you, which means it must be good. Of course, you have other urges as well, such as greed, envy, and anger, but these are not inspired by God, and acting out these emotions does not get you any closer to God. But the still, small voice is what you must listen to if you hope to become what you are truly meant to become.

"But you are more that this small voice.

"You are your feet that have traveled a million paths, searching for that one road that would lead to happiness, a secure life, and self-esteem. You have traveled many cities, looking for a friend, a lover, a guide. You are your feet that have been bruised and calloused on your journey. But also, you are the feet that are soft from a warm bath, that are washed by Jesus, that are fresh and new. Your feet have danced, next to the feet of the one you love. They have moved in time with the music and lifted your soul to heights of melody and harmony. You are your feet, and they will continue to carry you onward, despite the obstacles, despite their naked vulnerability to the elements and the thorns. You can trust your feet. They will keep you going.

"You are your legs, strong and agile. Your legs hold the memory of you as a child, running and playing with your family and the neighborhood kids. Your legs have grown with you, but still they know the joy of swimming at the community pool when you were six, and diving from the high dive your first time. Your legs may not be as beautiful in the eyes of men as someone else's, but beauty is not what legs are for. They are for walking peacefully next to your son, and for chasing your daughter about as she plays in the yard. Your legs will get stronger as you use them, just as your heart and mind will get stronger as you use them. Your legs were not made to lie about; they were made to take you where you must go.

"You are your hands, able to caress, hold, and touch lovingly. Your hands speak your intentions when you talk excitedly; they punctuate your sentences. With your hands, you can comfort the lonely, and teach the ignorant. You and your hands have much work to do. When it seems like you are lost in your thoughts, find something for your hands to do, and they will pull you out of yourself. They can create masterpieces in artistic expression. They can speak to the deaf. Your hands allow you to eat, to tie your shoelaces, to brush your hair, to write a quick message, to drive a car. Your hands are almost constantly in use. Think, if you said a word of thanks for every action your hands carried out, you would be in an unending state of praise!

"You are your mouth. You can say anything you want to say. Even the things that seem so difficult, like "I love you," or "I need your help," your mouth allows you to say. With your words, you can have your needs met. You can order meat at the grocery store, tell a cab driver where you need to go, ask a question in class, speak to a childhood friend. There is much that you need to say, and your mouth allows for all of it. You have the potential for nearly limitless expression, just because you have this one simple gift of speech. Your mouth serves only you. It is completely up to you what to say in every situation. Give thanks.

"You are your eyes. But more than this, you are also the interpretation of what you see. A common exercise in writing classes is to write about the room students are sitting in. They write two descriptive stories: one in a positive light and the other dark and gloomy. It is amazing that the same room is being described in each. This exercise shows us that (almost) everything does not have an inherent nature of good or bad, it is only people who cast a certain light on the subject. When I was depressed in Europe, I thought the place looked like a dungeon, with ancient stone work everywhere and dark alleyways that probably held people with knives and guns. Needless to say, when I first arrived in Europe, I was dazzled by the beauty of the very same city. Your eyes take in the facts and you interpret what those facts mean. You could see a homeless person as another example of our failed government and social services, or you could see him as an opportunity for you to help out and make a difference. A child could be a nuisance or a delight. An old woman is either a worn out old hag, or a crone with wisdom in her eyes. You can completely control your impressions of the world around you, even when you are depressed. Challenge yourself to find the good in the situations and people around you. No matter what they may seem at first glance, there is always a brighter way to look. Stop expecting that the world will change, for it is you that need to change. Either you wear bright glasses, or you wear dark ones, but be prepared to accept the feelings that will accompany your choice. Your eyes are your tools with which to change your thinking, and make it more positive. No matter what, you can always find a more positive way to look at things, even at major tragedies in your life. Your eyes were also given to you so that you could look inward. But see how distorted your gaze has become from so much regret and comparing to others! You cannot see the truth any longer. Which is why you have to start at the very beginning and try to see yourself not through your own eyes, not through the eyes of other people, but with God's eyes. His eyes are the most forgiving, most loving, most comforting eyes possible, and sometimes your own sight will only lead you down dark roads. Borrow His for a moment and see how brightly you shine.

"You are all these things, as well as being your heart, mind, and soul."

It was ironic and yet inspiring to read those words. Ultimately, on January 13, 2003, she did not follow her own advice. But that stark and disturbing truth does not negate the wisdom of her written words. She didn't need new words or different insights to ward off the impulse to pull the trigger that fateful and dishonorable Monday. She needed her medication to be effective and she needed to remember what she wrote a year and half earlier. Her words live beyond her death. Her suicide does not define her life, and her final act is not her finale. Her life outlives her tragic ending. Who she is and what she wrote destroys the bullet that took her from us. That last moment does not delete her previous moments. The curtain call to her life continues to this day.

Perhaps the hardest part of the trip to Tulsa was coming back home. The frantic activity of the previous week was over. Ginny returned to Princeton, and Kevin, Fran, and I returned to work. Routine life reemerged, though life without Karla, the "new normal," was anything but routine. I longed for a telephone call from her, just a brief call, telling us how she was doing. That call never comes.

11

Missing Her

From the day of her death until now, the word "grief" anchors my vocabulary. I experienced grief before, especially with the deaths of my dad, mom, sister and brother. I continue to miss them, all in different ways because my relationship with each of them was unique. Their deaths have changed me, and sorrow due to my loss is forever etched into my life.

But grief for Karla is different. The difference is not just a matter of degree; it isn't the same emotions felt more deeply. The dictionary maintains that grief is "an intense emotional suffering caused by loss, misfortune, injury, or evils of any kind." I can't argue with that definition, but it doesn't begin to capture my Karla-grief.

With her, I think of grief as a library, not just an emotion. It is a library that has large sections on all aspects of life: intellectual, social, physical, emotional, and spiritual. There are reference books, novels, poetry, history, religion, art, self-help, biography, etc. in each section. Karla-grief plunges me into every one of these aspects of life simultaneously, with all of that emotional, intellectual, social, physical, and spiritual data being downloaded into my being indiscriminately. It's grief-mania. It is overwhelming, and that is an understatement. Some days I don't know how I put one foot in front of the other, except that one foot happens to move first and the other follows, probably by habit.

I don't think I ever became clinically depressed, although I have no idea what my serotonin levels are. I toyed with the idea of asking the doctor to give me something to make sure my grief didn't totally absorb me, but I'm reluctant to take mood-altering medications. Karla needed them, and I saw what some of the side effects were and how difficult it was to get the right prescription in the proper amounts. I appreciate how valuable these drugs are for some people, but I also know that I over-respond to this kind of medication. One pain pill, for example, will mess up my thinking and equilibrium for days.

So far, I've been able to get by without taking antidepressants. My feet, sometimes beginning with the right one and sometimes the left one, mysteriously get me to where I need to go and do what I need to do. I distinctly remember Karla describing her depression in terms of wanting, no needing, to stay in bed. One Saturday afternoon I took a nap and briefly felt that attraction, but two hours later, I simply had to get up. I make no promises about the future (the worst may still be coming!!), but up to now I have dodged clinical depression.

Karla-Grief

Karla-grief hides within all my thoughts, a subtext that carries on its own dialogue regardless of what else I am thinking about. Sometimes at work or on the phone, I will make a reference to her even when it has nothing to do with the current conversation. I then realize that my secondary thoughts slipped into my primary thoughts. Sometimes I pay more attention to the subtext than to the conversation I am having or the other thoughts I am having. I don't know if it's unusual, but I am conscious of thinking on two levels quite clearly. I could be in a Diocesan Department Directors meeting with the Bishop, follow that conversation, make contributions to the discussion and simultaneously think about Karla in very specific ways. I don't remember being able to do that with any other subject or person prior to her death. I don't consider that ability a gift; it's more of an intrusion, and I attribute it to Karla-grief.

My emotional life lost its center. I thought I was pretty stable emotionally—usually having appropriate feelings at appropriate levels at appropriate times. Mad, glad, and sad all had their rightfully assigned duties and they were functioning—appropriately. Most of the time. In any case, I was relatively pleased with my emotional life. Now, it is emotional chaos. It isn't that I am completely out of control and at the mercy of raging and conflicting feelings. It isn't even that I cry and sob much more than I used to. (At one point, I seriously wondered how my body, my eyes in particular, could manufacture that many tears. Was my grief out-pacing my biological ability to create those tears? How does that happen, anyway?) It's more that I lost confidence in my ability to respond appropriately to any given situation. Mad, glad and sad are not fulfilling their rightful tasks. A lot of sad mingles in with glad. And mad shows up anywhere, at any time. Sad has arrogantly moved to center stage and will not relinquish his time even though he knows the cues for glad and mad. Emotional chaos follows, even though I somehow keep going, and most people are not aware of the quiet struggle I have to get those three key emotions back into their own rooms.

Karla-grief also infiltrates my social life. Outside of family and a few friends, I'm not too interested in doing anything or going anywhere with others. It seems like too much energy and work to socialize. I have done it, but my heart isn't in it like it used to be. I find myself more attracted to the anonymity of a dark movie theater (going alone is just fine) or a casino where the up and down feelings of expectation, followed usually by disappointment, with the occasional elation of winning, are delicious diversions. But that, too, is done alone—at least playing the video poker that I prefer. I thought I might be prone to vegetating in front of the TV, but that is surprisingly not helpful. I know because I tried. In any case, being alone is more attractive than socializing or meeting in groups. When I am alone, I can be with Karla without distractions.

Physically, I actually lost some useless weight since she died. Initially, I just didn't eat much, but more recently, I am deliberately dieting. I definitely needed to lose the pounds, but I confess that the diet is more than weight loss; it's also about tying to get control of my life. Maybe if I can rein in my weight problem, I can also rein in my Karla-grief. A gimmick. But it can't hurt me. On the other hand, for months I wasn't able to motivate myself to do the physical exercise I needed for my general health and for my grief. Many of the books I read encourage grievers to exercise regularly. That is a good idea, but I just couldn't get myself to do it.

Then I had an unexpected opportunity to spend four days in Naples, FL, with Fr. Bill. The slower pace, a few rounds of golf, a daily walk, pleasant conversations, delightful dining, and evenings on the beach watching God set Their sun while sipping a Rob Roy was enough to motivate me to walk our neighborhood for a half-hour each morning. I feel that little exercise gradually helping me heal, stretching and cleansing my spirit as it moves my muscles and energizes my blood. Maybe in time I will do forty-five minutes.

My spiritual life is also being hammered by her death. Many people get angry at God for allowing something like this to happen. I never felt that way. The God I believe in doesn't act that way. They (Father, Son, and Holy Spirit) love Karla, forgive her sins, and never interfered with her free will or the natural consequences of human behavior. My spiritual issues are not related to God but to me. I do pray, but not regularly enough. My meditation time becomes conscious "Karla time," and while I know that God hears whatever is in and on my heart, I drift away into a sadness that feels like self-pity. I trust that God is with me in this tough time, but I'm not sure I am with Them. Fr. Bill continues to be a great help, and we meet over a pecan chicken tender salad at O'Charley's almost weekly.

For Fran it is very difficult to attend our parish Mass because it brings back too many memories of Karla's funeral. I react differently and I participate every Sunday, but there are times when I can't do much but be there. Occasionally, my usual singing with gusto turns into an almost silent whimper. Where my Karla-grief spiritual life is headed I don't know. The spiritual life is always a journey, but this is a path I didn't expect or know anything about. Out of my grief, I simply trust that God will take care of me, even if I can't or don't take care of myself.

Life Goes On—Regardless

Life does go on, whether I'm ready or not, and that movement helps heal. My work helps me heal, not just because it gives me something to do with responsibilities I am constitutionally unable to ignore. It helps also because I enjoy what I do at work; it is challenging and rewarding, and I do it with a wonderful group of people. Fran and I support one another and have become even closer throughout these first few years, even though we both read in a number of books that 70% of marriages break up after the death of a child. We grieve differently, but at a very elemental level, we recognize that, as Karla's parents, we share a unique relationship with each other and with her. My relationship with Kevin has also deepened. We share more. Our mutual pain mingles and that mixture generates some comfort, love, and respect. Holidays and birthdays are especially difficult, but we are still family, and we are committed to staying close to each other.

It helps a little, too, when the Cardinals or Rams win a game, the Middle East seems a little closer to relative peace, the stock market goes up, the terrorists don't kill someone, the sun shines, the two Karla memorial gardens in our front yard bloom, friends and relatives call on the phone, I share a special meal, and I write this book. The rhythm of life helps heal. Very slowly. I sense that happening. But I don't know where I am on the healing scale. I do know that Karla-grief still has a tight hold on me.

It is, then, a library of grief, impacting much more than my emotional life. My thinking, perspective, and view of everything are now changed. My energy level is weakened. My values are rearranged. My goals are modified. My expectations are permanently altered. Along with Karla-grief, there are a few other things in life that have this profound and extensive impact. Genuine love does it. So does birth. A life-altering spiritual conversion also qualifies. But that's about it. Everything else is a relative molehill.

Many friends and relatives have sent us books, articles, prayers, and pamphlets on coping with grief. I have not read all of them, but eventually I probably will. They are helpful. The basic messages are there: it's okay to grieve at your own pace; everyone grieves differently; don't be ashamed of any of it; let it happen naturally; it does get better; regrets are ultimately useless—or, worse, destructive. Since that day I stood in the bedroom where she died, I keep thinking "Karla, you didn't have to do this." She didn't do it, her illness did. And, as Fr. Bill said in his final comments at the cemetery, "She is not her illness; she is much larger than her illness."

Strangely, the book that has brought me the most consolation so far is neither a grief book nor an overtly spiritual book. It is titled *The Noonday Demon*, written by Andrew Solomon with a subtitle "An Atlas of Depression," which is an apt description. Besides being well written, it is both a memoir and thoroughly researched. I needed to know more about her illness, why and how it killed her. This book provided an answer, at least enough of an answer to satisfy a significant part of my current question. It took me months to finish it because it was thought-provoking and I couldn't think quickly enough. There were times when I let it rest for days before I continued. But it touched me on many levels, and I am grateful that our friend Rosemary, sent it and that I wasn't intimidated by its size. At some point, I will read it again.

Regrets

Everyone tells me, and all the books reinforce it, that regrets are useless. They will hinder healing, feed the grief and open the door to depression. That's probably true. I try to ignore my regrets when they flash naked across my mind. I don't want to dwell on them because there is nothing I can do about past decisions or words or actions taken or not taken. "Deal with the present; accept that she is dead. Permanently dead, gone, never to be heard or seen in this life again. Remind yourself of the twenty-six years you had her. There's nothing you could have done to change the ultimate tragedy." That's what I tell myself.

Usually. But the fleeting regrets don't just go away. There are a series of "what if's," "why didn't I's," "I should have's," "I could have's," and the simple admissions that I was too dumb to pick up a danger signal that weekend before she died. For example, why didn't I go to Tulsa that weekend? We didn't want her to be released from the hospital, we knew it was a dangerous time, we knew she was pregnant, we knew she was not monitored, we knew she was intending to enroll in school and that it might be complicated, we knew she had suicidal thoughts within the past week. Knowing all that, why in the hell didn't I just get on an airplane, spend the weekend with her, help her get enrolled and support her regardless of what happened? That would have been simple enough. If I did that, she probably would be alive today. Now *that's* a regret worthy of sleepless nights and fitful days!

Here's another one: I should have known that she would have been safer here with us. Of course, she could have committed suicide in our house, too. And that might even have been harder on us. But as things turned out, I now wish I had made a stronger case for keeping her home with us. Maybe she would have made it through January and then for many years to come.

And here are some more regrets:

- If I had insisted that she call me before she would ever attempt suicide again, she might have called. I might have been able to stall her, talk her out of it. Maybe before she pulled the trigger, she would have remembered her promise and made the call.

- I should have realized that she had too much going on: coming out of depression, being released from the hospital, having a baby, moving into Madonna House, going back to school, readjusting to Tulsa, quitting her job, rebounding from relationships in Stillwater—it was all too much. She was in no condition to handle all of that. I should have helped simplify her life, probably by discouraging her from going to school that semester and assuring her that she didn't have to get a job. Maybe she could have made it with a little less pressure on her.

- I should have anticipated possible enrollment problems. Or that she was simply not capable of going to school that semester. I was with her in August when she enrolled, and I experienced complications with registration then. Why did I assume that it would be an easy process in Tulsa? Why did I assume she could deal with it without stress? I should have known better and called the school myself.

- I should have called Tulsa Center for Behavioral Health that Sunday when we discovered that she had morning sickness and insisted that they contact her regarding her medication. Instead, we called her and assumed that she would take care of it. Her ability to deal with complications at that time was impaired. Why didn't I know that and act on it?

If I keep thinking about it, I'm sure I could list many more regrets, not only related to that weekend, but to many years of decision-making with her and her illness.

We all have regrets; in fact, to be human means to have regrets. I have other regrets in life: things I have done and not done, relationships that I let drop, decisions I have made, projects that I didn't follow through on, books I haven't read—the list goes on and on. Throughout most of my life, I've dealt with these regrets pretty well: acknowledge them and then let them go. Chalk it up to experience and try to learn from them. Don't let them linger and interfere with my present reality. I don't want to suppress them; I usually just admit them and move on. I am not guilt-ridden.

I want to do the same with my Karla-regrets. Maybe in time, I will get there. Maybe it's still too early. All I can say right now is that these regrets have not gone away, and my grief will not let me ignore them.

Who to Blame?

Actually, regret is a euphemism for blame. Regret implies remorse and disappointment while blame includes responsibility, guilt, and fault. Somewhere in the house of regret lives the feeling of fault. Whom do I blame for Karla's suicide? The best answer, of course, is to blame no one or anything (except her illness). Blame, like regret, is useless. And at some point, I predict that I will be able to honestly come to that position. But I'm not there yet.

Right now there's plenty of blame for everyone. I blame myself for not doing more; I blame us as a family for not protecting her better that final weekend; I blame Lonnie for needing a gun; I blame Karla for something I can't pin down—not for her illness, but for something indiscriminate that lies between her bipolar disorder and her personal responsibility; I certainly blame the hospital for releasing her too soon; I blame Justin for hindering her recovery; I blame the father of her child for taking advantage of her; I blame society for not understanding mental illness and for allowing a two-tier treatment approach—one for the rich and an inferior one for the poor; I blame insurance companies for not covering mental illness for college students; I blame … I blame … I blame. There's plenty of blame to go around, and I know that if I nurture this blame, give it more time and energy, allow it to develop theories and long lists of accusations, seek more details to support my instincts and talk about it more, I will be very angry and spend the rest of my life seeking revenge.

I choose not to live the rest of my life with blame, anger, revenge, depression, and rage at the core of my emotional life. On the other hand, I don't want to dismiss these feelings too abruptly either. Part of grieving is resolving these emotions. I am convinced that acceptance and peace are possible, even in a situation like Karla's suicide. But it is not easy or simple.

In fact, even stating my regrets and admitting my impulse to blame is dangerous. Saying it out loud, writing it publicly, and admitting it to other people gives life to the feelings. Karla told us on Christmas night that she was reluctant to talk about the destructive messages she was getting from the "demons" in her head because telling us would add another depth of reality to the voices. She was concerned that reporting them to another person would make matters worse. This hesitation to speak out was contrary to her basic nature, contradicts the conventional wisdom that encourages people to "open up" (the whole counseling profession is based on this premise), and, ultimately, she did share her "demons" with us.

But her hesitation has some truth in it. Maybe some things are best left unsaid. For example, if you tell someone like an acquaintance or co-worker the absolute truth that "I don't like you," that honesty will end the civil relationship you have with that person. Most people wisely judge that in a situation like that, they simply don't say anything about their true feelings to that person. On the other end of the spectrum, if you are attracted to a co-worker or acquaintance and, in fact, love that person but you know that pursuing a deeper relationship is unwise, it is best that you don't say "I love you." Saying those words with conviction moves the relationship to a more complicated and usually dangerous level. Most mature people don't say those words.

That was Karla's point when she reluctantly told us about her demons on Christmas night. That's also my point right now about admitting my regrets and blame. Obviously, I decided to include these remarks and thereby give them more status, but I do so reluctantly and with the conviction that these regrets and the blame will not consume me, that I am relatively confident that in the long run, acceptance and peace will predominate. In any case, these feelings are huge waves in the ocean of missing her.

I Simply Miss Her

That's it—I simply miss her. I miss her smile: she was a beautiful young woman, 5'4", weighed around 115 pounds, good figure, strikingly blue eyes, high cheekbones, and gorgeous, long blond hair. Her smile lit up her whole being and doubled her attractiveness. I want to see that smile again—not in a picture or video—but on her face, reflecting her spirit.

I miss her enthusiasm and passion: she was never bland. She had definite ideas and opinions. She was decidedly liberal and progressive in politics, religion, and social policy and did not hesitate to express her opinions with conviction. She was antiwar, even helping to organize and speak at a peace rally on the OSU campus in the fall of 2002. We didn't always agree, but I miss just sitting back and watching her in an animated discussion, stating her position clearly and articulately. Sometimes I would just marvel at her commitment, knowledge, and enthusiasm and just say to myself: "Go, girl!" She made me proud, even when I didn't agree with her.

I miss our conversations: we talked often—on many levels, some like the animated debates I just mentioned, but usually more intimate and personal. We talked about books, ideas, philosophy, religion, history, relationships, family, school, work, my writing, her writing, even sports occasionally. Talk is the air of relationships and we often breathed the same air. My air is stale without her.

I miss her personality: we are all unique, but being unique was a deliberate and deep-seated motivation for her. In many ways, the profile of her in this book reflects the impact of her illness on her personality. We knew her before bipolar attacked her and when that disorder was "ordered." Kevin described her real personality in his tribute to her at the wake service. That's what I miss every day.

I miss being there when she and Kevin were together: just watching them relate, sometimes bantering, sometimes serious just filled me with awe. I so delighted in each of them separately, but there was an added thrill when they were together. It made a daddy proud, and it played a perfectly tuned, soothing, musical cord in me that resonated throughout my being.

I miss her relationship with Fran: it was a beautiful blending of that mysterious mother-daughter thing that we men generally don't get. Consignment store shopping, cooking, advice sharing, dominoes, hair, fashion, relationships—all those things that the two of them had almost automatically. It was fun to see it and witness it, even though it was usually beyond me.

I miss her career: I always enjoyed discussing her classes with her, and I believed she would eventually wind up as a counselor, teacher, or some other helping professional. If she had continued her education to get a Masters and then a PhD (which she thought about), then it would have been fun following that path with her. Eventually she would have decided on a career, and I looked forward to learning about her job. Regardless of whatever other career choices she would have made, she undoubtedly would have continued writing, and I already miss all those conversations about her writing as well.

I miss her family: at some point, she would have married. I miss a son-in-law, and I miss her children, my grandchildren. I know they don't exist, but now, they will never exist. I miss the idea and the dream of having grandchildren through her and her husband. I looked forward to her little kids, their birthday parties, Thanksgiving, Christmas, and one of Karla's favorite holidays—the fourth of July. It would have been a glorious part of my twilight years.

I miss her graduation from college and her wedding: two events that would have been great celebrations.

In other words, I miss what would have been. All those dreams were deeply ingrained, and it's now almost impossible to rip them out of me. They are so sharp, with jagged edges, varying sizes and attached to the tender lining of my spirit. Removing these dreams and expectations causes spiritual and emotional hemorrhages. So far, I haven't been able to stop the bleeding.

Missing her is the nucleus of my grief.

All Grief is Unique

Actually, there is no such thing as "grief." There are only grievers. Everyone grieves in his or her own way, within the circumstances of his or her life and experience. To try to describe this grief in generic, universal terms tears that grief from its personal, most painful roots, like pulling a wisdom tooth without an anesthetic. All grief is ultimately and eternally individual. No one suffers grief exactly like I do—or you do.

There is no such thing as love either. There are only lovers. Each love relationship is unique. It is precisely the particularity of each love relationship that makes love real. Love for parents is real but different with each parent. Love for children is intense but varies with each child. Love for friends changes with each friend. You could be married to five husbands or wives and each marriage would be unique. Love does not exist in the abstract; it only exists in the concrete, specific, diversified, specialized world of individual relationships.

We talk about love and grief in general, but we don't experience them in general. That's why the poets, philosophers, psychologists, and preachers have an impossible task when they try to define, or even describe, these (and many other) experiences. In the final analysis, it simply can't be done. Ultimately, we are alone.

Fortunately, life doesn't end with aloneness. We do connect with one another in varying ways. We are social by nature. We do communicate on multiple levels, sometimes poorly and sometimes well, and, fortunately again, we are able to express our experiences efficiently enough to reach some degree of reliability in our communication with one another. Without this ability to connect, we would despair. Most of us accept this truth intuitively. Many of those who lose this intuition because of chemical imbalance, destructive thinking, or extreme circumstances commit suicide. Fortunately once again, there aren't more of these people. Unfortunately, Karla was one of them.

The stark reality of our ultimate uniqueness mingles with our accompanying gift to communicate effectively. This book reflects more the former than the latter. The presumption here is that our family story is best communicated to you by maintaining the personal, individual, specific, unique nature of the four of us, and how bipolar disorder and suicide burst unwelcome into our home. I have deliberately avoided universalizing our experience because any life experience is more authentic and honest when described personally and individually.

However, I suspect that our experience is similar to some of your experiences. As you read our story, I invite you to search your own feelings and history for your experience of frustration, powerlessness, expectations denied, confusion, regret, shock, loss, grief, love, devotion, sacrifice, and the mystery of family. While the circumstances of your life and our life may not appear similar on the surface, I believe we share many of the same feelings. Our story does intersect with your story. Go to that place in your life where you have felt most abandoned or helpless, and you will find the Smith family in the same neighborhood. Recall your most difficult time and we will also be there, not experiencing your troubles, but standing near you experiencing our troubles. While you remember these sad times, also relive the recovery, the hope, the victory after suffering, the peace within the chaos. We will be there, too.

The hope is that as you read about us, you can connect with yourself. If we offer you an honest and gripping account of our struggles, acceptance, and peace, we pray that our description leads you through our story into your own story. When that journey takes place, the uniqueness of our experience meshes with the uniqueness of your experience, and genuine sharing evolves out of the process.

This book, then, is not about the Smiths; it is about all of us, finding connections with one another even as we enjoy our uniqueness.

Those connections happen regularly. The three of us have been quite public about Karla's bipolar disorder, her suicide and our grief. Interviews in a number of local newspapers, participation in support groups and mental illness conferences, articles in a newsletter, references to bipolar, suicide and grief at workshops and meetings, and honest conversations with people continue to encourage people to tell us their stories. It is amazing how many people are personally affected by mental illness and suicide. We tell our story publicly (as in this book) in order to raise awareness among all people and to offer whatever comfort we can to those who suffer. It is also a way for us to receive comfort and healing. We do not have answers, but we have our experience to share. Karla would want us to do that.

Suicide Awareness

I am also more aware of suicides. It happens more often than most people even imagine.

"Suicide is a serious public health challenge that has not received the attention and degree of national priority it deserves. Many Americans are unaware of suicide's toll and its global impact. It is the leading cause of violent deaths worldwide, outnumbering homicide or war-related deaths.

"In the U.S., suicide claims approximately 30,000 lives each year. Overall, suicide was the 11th leading cause of death among Americans in 2000. In 1999, more that 152,000 hospital admissions and more than 700,000 visits to hospital emergency rooms were for self-harming behaviors. The vast majority of all people who die by suicide have a mental illness—often undiagnosed or untreated.

"Suicide was also the fourth leading cause of death among youth aged 10–14, third among those between 15 and 24, second among 25 to 34 year olds, and fourth among those 35–44 years in 1999. The rate of suicide is highest among older men, compared with all other age groups. But alarmingly, the rate of teen suicide (for those from ages 15 to 19) has tripled since the 1950s."

("Achieving the Promise: Transforming Mental Health Care in America", Final Report, The President's New Freedom Commission on Mental Health, July 2003.)

This tragic data seldom makes the headlines. What does make the headlines almost daily are the reports of suicide bombers, people who use their own death as a weapon against presumed enemies. Suicide has become a tactical strategy to effect political change or to gain a battleground advantage. It took me some time to identify why this tactic infuriates me—even more so than the common outrage at this barbaric behavior.

Suicide bombers divert public attention from the tragedy of individuals who take their own lives for nonpolitical reasons. Gradually "suicide" and "bomber" go together in the public consciousness; people automatically and subconsciously connect suicide with bomber. That inference carries the connotation of guilt, terrorist, fanatic, and "deserving to die." With that kind of word association it is even harder to talk about "regular" suicide, its tragic causes and wrenching impact. My daughter was not a "suicide bomber," and I resent even sharing the word with them.

The Possibility of Peace

Ultimately, anger, grief, frustration, and powerlessness are supposed to lead to acceptance and peace. Good idea! What I have learned so far is that this passage takes a long time. Sometimes, I feel like I did the night of January 13, 2003, when the muscular officer from the Shiloh police department told me Karla had died. The shock is still there lurking in the shadows of my soul. It's all still there: the pain, disbelief, loss, confusion, anger, and a constant weariness that erodes my being. I want it all to go away. Just go away. Leave me alone. But it lingers—confident that I can't chase it away. And I can't.

Bad as it is at times, I do not experience despair. Occasionally, I have a good time. In the past, I was basically happy and optimistic with periodic downtimes. Now my downtimes surround my periodic good times. I want to get back to the original formula. That will take a big dose of faith and acceptance.

My faith provides a context for my acceptance. People who do not believe in a God or an afterlife also suffer from loss, and they, too, experience the many faces of grief. Apparently, they get through their grief without a faith reference. I sincerely wish them well, and, as far as I know, I share many of their convictions and can learn much about life and death from them.

But my personal story includes my faith, in life as well as in Karla's death. My faith does not take away my pain—obviously. But my belief in a loving, compassionate God, an afterlife called heaven, a union between the living and the dead, and a continuing existence for Karla and for me after I die, colors the way I handle my grief. I don't compare my life with anyone else, and I certainly don't judge or even compete with anyone else's belief or disbelief. I simply state that, for me, my faith provides a context of consolation and meaning for my life and for death. I don't believe these things about life and death so that they bring me consolation in a difficult time. I believe them because I trust that they are true—they represent reality at its deepest level. Incidentally, they are also consoling, but that consolation is not based on my need to be comforted. It is based on my conviction that that is the way things are.

This faith helps me accept things in life, and in death.

Accepting something is very different from admitting something. I admit that Karla has died, although admission is not as automatic as it sounds. I knew immediately when I heard it that she had died. It took basically the next week, the wake service, the funeral and the burial to really admit that she was permanently gone. To admit that stark reality is merely an intellectual conclusion. It is a true statement. I admit it.

But I still don't accept it. Acceptance gathers all the negative emotions, the weary-making thoughts and half-thoughts, the impulses that sabotage peace and the barely resistible pull into self-pity into one manageable ball of pain and then throws it into the harbor at the foot of Paradise Point where it dissolves in the gently ebbing waters of peace. Acceptance absorbs the pain and transforms it into serenity. Acceptance infiltrates every pore and cleanses each one, thoroughly and individually, from the inside out, until each one breathes cleaner, deeper, and healthier.

I know what acceptance feels like because I have experienced it in other areas of my life. I have also experienced it in fleeting moments in regard to Karla's death. I've had a few glimpses of genuine acceptance and the peace it delivers. But it doesn't last—the weight of the loss drags me down and before long, the acceptance escapes. In time, I trust that acceptance will be a friend who stays with me longer. I miss her. I will always miss her. I want to always miss her. But I want to accept missing her. Some day I will.

12

Paradise Point 2003

Paradise Point is one of the experiences that nudge me in the direction of acceptance and peace.

I believe it was sometime in April 2003, that Fran and I talked about a summer vacation. I was in the mood for something very low key, a getaway place with little stimulation and time to read and try to relax. She wanted to do another cruise. I was reluctant. There were too many memories of the family cruise the previous July. It was the last time Karla was "normal" with the four of us. It was too joyous—the Smith family together, talking, laughing, enjoying each other and the activities we did. I didn't think I could face that same kind of experience this soon. Besides, the itinerary again included St. Thomas and Paradise Point. We discussed it often, and I really don't know when or how I agreed, but somewhere along the way, I consented.

We invited our friend Margie, to join us. She and Fran had become good friends, including jigsaw puzzle buddies, since Karla died, and I have known Margie for many years through church activities. She also helped with focus. I figured I couldn't get too morose about Karla with a first-time cruiser in our group. This time Fran and I got a cabin with a balcony while Margie took an inside stateroom. I was able to have my necessary, quiet, alone time even amid all the frivolity, entertainment, and activities of the ship and the ports of call. It worked out fine, but I was apprehensive about the whole thing, and in particular about Paradise Point. It was too raw a wound to expose myself to the predicted pain. But I agreed to go.

This time, St. Thomas and Paradise Point was the first stop on the cruise. We sailed into the now-familiar harbor, and the three of us rode to the top of Flag Hill. During the two previous trips, I noticed a sign indicating a nature trail behind the café that went a quarter of a mile higher up the hill, but I never went there on the first two trips. This year I did, and it was there, alone, on a bench along that isolated trail when I consciously begged that the peace of Paradise Point would seep into my troubled soul, caress the memory of Karla, surround the grief, and cure my pain. I felt the disappointment of the previous summer when Karla didn't connect with my reaction to Paradise Point. I recalled the mania of last fall and the depression of December. I lingered on her hospital stay and finally her suicide, wake, and funeral. I easily felt the continuing pain of my Karla-grief. I sought relief.

Somewhere in my heart I knew that God was the ultimate origin of my continuing reaction to Paradise Point, but my immediate response to the place consumed my attention. I sat there for quite awhile. There was no miracle of healing. There was no spectacular release of my Karla-grief. But as I walked back down the trail to join Fran and Margie for the final act of a trained bird show, I was aware of some slight change in me.

Fran and I hugged and shed a few more tears. A vendor selling a cooling cloth that goes around the neck of a heat victim asked if we were okay. Yes, we were, but I wished for an instant that someone would invent a similar device for healing a grieving soul. As we descended the hill, as we boarded the ship and got dressed for dinner, and as we sat quietly on our balcony, it slowly dawned on me what Paradise Point had done for me that day. It assured me that there is a possibility of peace, that acceptance may one day be mine, that her loss might not hurt so deeply forever. That day may come. It could happen. Paradise Point said so.

At dinner that evening we shared our day. The Utz's were our dinner companions. Joe and Kathy, their son Chris, and their daughter Kathryn, with her husband, Paul, joined the three of us for dinner each evening. Chris, Kathryn, and Paul were about the same age as Kevin and Karla had been the previous cruise. The age similarity reinforced the memories of our family cruise. The Utz's were a delightful family and I truly enjoyed our meals together. I told them the first night about Karla as we introduced ourselves and talked about our expectations of the cruise. I was not like the three thousand other people on board; I was on a personal pilgrimage to Paradise Point.

When Joe asked how our day went, I simply replied that I went to Paradise Point and the rest of the cruise was all downhill. I knew then, and it is reinforced now, that I don't need to return to Paradise Point in the near future—or ever. I've been there, and I now carry the Point within me.

My experience of Paradise Point is a thread of acceptance and peace that gets brighter and more prominent as the Smith family tapestry gradually unfolds. Fran and Kevin's threads are different colors, creating unique patterns, but we remain one tapestry. And the colors, shapes, texture, and designs that are Karla's continue to weave in and out of our patterns as we create and unfold our family story. Our tapestry lives.

Epilogue

On December 13, 2003, Oklahoma State University, at Kevin's request, granted a posthumous bachelor of arts degree in English to Karla. She was just three courses away from graduation when she died. It was a tearful but joyous occasion. In her comments to the thousands of people attending the graduation, Dr. Carol Moder, associate professor and head of the department of English, said, "Karla was an outstanding student, with a great passion for the life of the mind. For Karla, words and ideas were dynamically charged living entities. Her intense approach to thinking and to living emerged from deep ethical, emotional, spiritual, and intellectual commitments. Karla was a promising scholar, a sensitive reader, a dazzling conversationalist, and a committed and original writer whose creative works are marked by a generosity to others and to a rigorous self-scrutiny." We couldn't agree more, and we are deeply grateful to OSU for bestowing this long-awaited and much-desired degree to Karla. The degree, now part of a collage—a Christmas 2003 gift from Kevin—containing mementos of Karla's graduation ceremony, hangs proudly in the hallway of our home.

As *The Tattered Tapestry* demonstrates, Karla was always open about her bipolar illness. She talked about it freely and wrote extensively about her experiences and feelings. She was usually less communicative when depressed, but even then she often kept a journal and shared some of what her world was like. She was a communicator.

We want to emulate her openness. The three of us (Kevin, Fran, and Tom) are comfortable speaking to groups and sharing our experiences. In January of 2004, Kevin was the keynote speaker for a mental health conference sponsored by the United Methodist Church of Shiloh, Illinois. A few months later, Tom spoke at the annual clergy and healthcare professionals' conference, "Suicide: Preventing the Irreversible," at St. Elizabeth's Hospital in Belleville, Illinois. In June 2004, Kevin presented a moving tribute to Karla at their ten-year high school class reunion in Tulsa, Oklahoma. In August, Fran was the guest speaker for the Depression and Bipolar Support Alliance in Belleville. In October of 2004, Tom preached at an Ecumenical Prayer Service during Mental Illness Awareness Week. His talk was later published in the Spring 2005 issue of *Human Development*. As time progresses, we continue making similar presentations, and we welcome future opportunities to share our story publicly.

All past presentations, newspaper articles, and candles of hope in memory of Karla can be found at www.InMemoryOfKarla Smith.com.

As a result of this public testimony, thousands of people have heard or read our story. Initially we were amazed at the number of people who talked to us personally about family members who suffered from bipolar disorder, depression, schizophrenia, or other mental illnesses or died by suicide. The people who talk to us always appreciate our openness about our experience. We have come to expect this response when we share our story.

Coupled with this kind of response is our desire to help people who are close to those who suffer from mental health problems or who have lost a loved one to suicide. We believe that some good can come out of our tragedy, not only for us but for other people as well. Our loss and our grief are permanent. But we have also learned from our suffering and will continue to learn for the rest of our lives. We looked for a way to share our story and what we have learned at this point. We know there are millions of people who struggle with mental illness and millions more who love someone with a mental illness. We are convinced that together we can lessen the pain caused by mental health problems and suicide.

After much discussion and prayer, we decided to create the Karla Smith Foundation (KSF). We believe that KSF, along with other support groups, alliances, advocacy organizations, and agencies, both public and private, will provide a significant additional service to the families and friends of people with mental health problems.

We have our mission: the Karla Smith Foundation provides hope for a balanced life to family and friends of anyone with a mental illness or who lost a loved one to suicide. "Hope for a Balanced Life" is our motto. Mental illness and suicide create an imbalance in the emotional, mental, and behavioral lives of sufferers' families and friends. Most often they are confused and frustrated by the behavior of their loved ones. Their own lives are unpredictable and unsteady, and they see little hope for "normal" lives again. They long for balance and the opportunity to live lives untouched by mental illness or suicide. But they see no end to painful situations that they cannot control.

The founders of KSF know that there is hope for a balanced life even when there is untreated mental illness in the family, even when a suicide has occurred. KSF helps discover and nurture that hope.

Support groups, public education and awareness, resources, and an interactive Web site are all services currently sponsored by KSF. We will continue to expand KSF as the needs emerge and the funding develops.

To contact KSF, write, call, or e-mail:

Karla Smith Foundation
10101 West Main Street
Belleville, IL 62223
1-888-KSF-HOPE (1-888-573-4673)
1-618-624-5771 (local)
E-mail: ksf@karlasmithfoundation.org
Web site: www.karlasmithfoundation.org

If you wish to contribute to this tax-exempt organization to help us accomplish our mission, please send your check to 10101 West

Main Street, Belleville, IL 62223 or contribute online at www.Karla
SmithFoundation.org.

On April 14, 2007, four years after Karla died, Kevin married
Emily Sherbert. Karla and Emily had been best childhood friends in
Broken Arrow, Oklahoma, from ages five through thirteen and our
two families had socialized together. Emily and Karla later went to
different high schools and colleges and lived in different cities, and
both families moved, so the contact between the childhood friends
and families became occasional. When Karla died, we put her obitu-
ary in the Tulsa paper; Emily's father read it and called Emily, who
was living in Kansas City. Emily drove from Kansas City to Belleville,
Illinois (near St. Louis), for the wake. When she came through the
receiving line, we didn't recognize her, but she and Kevin visited
briefly. Kevin happened to be assigned to a work project in Kansas
City at that time, and he and Emily met to talk about Karla. Four
years later they were happily married in St. Louis. Karla's death
brought them together as adults.

Every family is a tapestry, and every family tapestry is torn and tattered to some degree. The Smith family tapestry today is not what we
thought it would be when the twins joined us in 1976. There are rips
and tears in various parts of our tapestry; the two largest, of course,
result from Karla's bipolar disorder and suicide. But there are also
patches, places where new thread and twine fix the rips, tears, and
holes. And Karla remains a vital part of our expanding tapestry. Personally and through the Karla Smith Foundation, we are gradually
reweaving the tattered ends of thread, twine, and fabric that make up
our tapestry.

The mending of our tapestry blends with the much larger tapestry
that represents our whole society, in which mental illness and suicide
continue to rip and tear the peace and balance out of people's lives.
By gradually mending our family tapestry, we also help mend the hole
in the societal tapestry. By helping others through the Karla Smith
Foundation, we are sewing new thread and twine into the torn spots
in our world tapestry.

Hope does triumph over despair. Light does follow the darkness. Peace is possible even after emotional turmoil. It is our dream that the story of our tattered tapestry will bring this hope, light, and peace to each of you.

978-1-58348-385-5
1-58348-385-3

CPSIA information can be obtained at www.ICGtesting.com
Printed in the USA
LVOW121416200912

299619LV00001B/1/A